History of Nations

" From 300 B.C to 677 C.E "

2

Ibn al-Jawzi (1116 C.E -1200 C.E)

Alreshah.net

Canada

Alreshah
www.Alreshah.net

If any error is found, please contact us through our website alreshah.net.

Book Layout © 2017 BookDesignTemplates.com

History of Natioans 2 / Ibn al-Jawzi. -- 1st ed.
ISBN 978-1-989875-04-9

Contents

Introduction

In the name of God, The Entirely Merciful, the Especially Merciful

This is the translation of the first part in a sequence of books written by Imam Abd al-Raḥmān b. ʿAlī b. Muḥammad Abu 'l-Fara<u>sh</u> b. al-Jawzi, known as Ibn al-Jawzī. He was an Arab Muslim jurisconsult, preacher, orator, heresiographer, traditionist, historian, judge, hagiographer, and philologist who lived in Baghdad during the twelfth century.

In this book, he collected what was known in his time about the nation's history. As the reader will note, this book focused first on parts more toward the Middle East region and on the prophets known to Jews and Christians. The reason behind this is that Baghdad was the heart of the Islamic world, and most of the other nations' knowledge had been concentrated in Baghdad in the Golden Age of the Islamic Empire.

It is essential to understand that the first and second part of this book, until 600 AD, was based on what the Imam read and gathered from Israelites known to him in his time. So, similarities might be found between the historical events mentioned in those two parts and Biblical stories.

Starting from the end of the second book onward, the authentication differs hugely, as those are more related to Islamic history and the states surrounding the Islamic empire. The spread of knowledge and literacy within the Islamic world resulted in better record-keeping, and references to an event were recorded in different documents.

That what makes this book one of the important books in the history of the region, especially from 600 AD to the author's death, which will be in part three onward.

The tale of Zechariah(PBUH)

He is Zechariah son of Adi – it has been said son of Barkhiya- a descendent of Solomon, son of David (PBUH), Abu Huraira quoted the Messenger (PBUH) as saying: "Zechariah was a carpenter".

The tale of events in the time of Zechariah

The story of Hannah's vow, Faqudh's daughter. When she became pregnant she vowed to dedicate her son to the service of God in the temple. when she gave birth to Mary, she carried her to the worshippers, so they cast their pens as to who should be responsible for Mary, and Zechariah claimed right to guardianship over

Marry because she was niece of his wife Eesha. However, the scholars disputed his claim and every one had an argument in his own favor. Finally, the issue was decided by casting lots. All of them went to a nearby river and threw their pens into it. The pens went down the river, except the floating pen of Zechariah. Thus, it was decided in his favor and everyone conceded that Zechariah would be the guardian of Mary. He brought her and decided to build her a small chamber within the worship hall so that she may devote herself to God with concentration away from other people. She grew up in his care and he visited her on and off in her chamber where no one else was allowed to enter. Zechariah was astonished by something:

whenever visited her, he found with her sustenance which included fruits of all seasons. When he asked her how she got it, Mary said that she got it from God who gives sustenance to whomsoever He pleases as much as He pleases. Thus, Zechariah was convinced that she was chosen for a high station. Suddenly, he also longed for a child knowing that even in his old age, God can give him a child as he gave Mary fruit of season. Whereupon, Zechariah invoked his Lord to give him a child, his wife was named Eesha, daughter of Imran- she is Mary's sister- she gave birth to John, and asked for a sign for this great event and how near it was, so he is no longer able to speak except, praying God (Glory be to Him).

Al Rabi ibn Anas said: when Jews heard that Jesus spoke in the cradle, they become envious of Zechariah and became hostile to him and when he informed them that Mary is pregnant, they gossiped. When they found out this incident is written in the Torah and Solomon informed them of it, they sought Zechariah to kill him, however he ran forwards a tree to flee and avoid the enemies. Then, the trunk of the tree cracked and Zechariah entered in so that the cervices joined as before. Consequently, Satan gathered the people to the tree where Zechariah was hiding. He searched for him by putting his hand below the tree, asking people to split the tree into pieces. The people obeyed him, cutting the tree with a saw and killed him.

Al Suddy said: they accused Zechariah of being made Mary pregnant, so they sought him and he ran forward the tree.

Ahmed ibn Jaafar al Munady said that Zechariah was almost one hundred years.

The tale of John (PBUH)

It was said that John was born six months before Jesus.

It has been said that he was born before Jesus has been raised to heaven, and he had a great passion for knowledge when he was still a boy and he was endowed with righteousness even as a young man.

Qatada said regarding God's saying: "and we gave him judgment [while yet] a boy.'""19:12(."أتيناه الحكم صبيا), he has been three years old.

The biographers held that God inspired to John and gave him sacred scriptures from a young age, then he came to the Levant inviting people, and he was eating locusts and the leaves of the trees, and he used to weep copiously, fearing God, to the extent that his face was etched with the groove of his tears.

It was reported that his father Zechariah said to him: "I asked God (Glory be to Him) a son to be a delight for me. He replied:

"Oh father! Jibril told me that between the Heaven and Hell, there is only one crossing which cannot be crossed except by the tears of the weepers?" Zechariah then said: "weep my son," and they both wept together.

The tale of why John has been killed

It was reported by ibn Abbas that: Jesus sent John, son of Zechariah besides twelve of his disciples teaching people, they would prohibit marriage to the niece, the king at that time has a niece whom he was admired and he wanted to marry, and he used to fulfill what she wants every day. When her mother knew that, she said to her: when you come to the king and he would ask you what do you want, say: I would like the head of John, he said: anything other than that, she said: nothing else. He called John and brought his head in a washtub and a drop of his blood fell on the ground and continued to boil until God sent upon them Nebuchadnezzar and came to know about it from an old woman who belonged of the Israelites, he vowed to kill the Israelites to halt the boiling of blood. He killed seventy thousand people and the blood stopped boiling.

Another account says: there was a king in the children of Israel, he has a wife and a daughter whom he loved much. She used to request something every day. Her mother said to her: when he asks you what do you need: say: I'd like the head of John, son of

Zechariah, then he rebuke her so much and was furious with her, she got out. The surrounding hypocrites said to him: what John and the head of John! he said: bring her the head of John.

They came to him while he was standing in prayer in Geroon Church, Damascus, and beheaded and put it in a washtub and ordered to be given to his daughter. While she was in her way back to her mother, the earth swallowed her. When her mother knew that, she came out unveiling her face and the earth had swallowed her except her head, she said: cut off the head to be washed and enshrouded and she cried over her. Doing that, the earth ejected the body.

It was reported by Abdullah ibn Zubair that John, son of Zechariah was killed because of a prostitute, she was his neighbor.

It was reported by Abu Huraira and ibn Omar (may Allah be pleased with them): a woman named "Raba" killed John son of Zechariah, and brought his head in a washtub, then the earth swallowed her.

Abdullah ibn Umar said: seventy of Apostles were killed by this woman in one day. She was described in the Torah as "the killer of the Apostles, and she is going to be on a pulpit of fire that the inhabitants of Hell will hear her cries.

It was reported by Urwa ibn Zubair this woman named "Azbeel", she had killed seventy of the apostles, and John son of Zechariah was the last.

Fatima reported that the Prophet (PBUH) said: "John son of Zechariah stayed with the children of Israel forty years".

Qatada said: he was killed in Damascus.

The tale of punishment of the children of Israel for killing John son of Zechariah

The Prophet(PBUH) said: "the worldly life is worthless in the sight of God, that John son of Zechariah has been killed by a woman".

Al Suddy reported his scholars saying that a man saw in a dream that Jerusalem would be ruined and the children of Israel would be destroyed by a Babylonian orphan boy, son of a widow, named "Nebuchadnezzar", so he sought him until he found his mother cutting wood in the forests and selling it. He then came, talked to him and gave him three dirhams to buy some food. In the second day, he did the same, and so on the third day, then he said to him: when you came to the throne, give me a warrant of safety. He said: are you mocking at me?!He said: No, but do a favor for me. His mother said to him: never mind, you wouldn't lose anything. He wrote it and handed it over to him, then he said: what would you do if I came to you and the people around you stopped me, so make for me a sign to recognize me. He said tie the warrant of safety on a staff and raised it up.

When John was killed and his blood continued to boil until the time Nebuchadnezzar entered Jerusalem. It did not stop even though and was thrown over it. It was the blood of John son of Zechariah, and Nebuchadnezzar went on to conquer the Israelites, they became entrenched with their places so that he was about to retreat, however, an Israeli old woman came and said to him: if I opened the city for you, you give me what I want and kill whomsoever I ask you to kill, and abstain whenever ask you? He said: yes. She said: in the early morning, divide your soldiers into four squads, then keep a squad on every part of the city, then raise your hands to the heaven and say: O God, we ask you by the blood of John, son of Zechariah to open the city. Doing that, the city was opened and they entered from everywhere. She said: fight around this blood until it stop gushing, so he killed seventy thousand people of the Israelites. When the blood stopped to gush out, she said cease killing, since if a prophet has been killed, God would take revenge of the killers and those who approved killing him.

The owner of the warrant came to him and he assured protection to him and his household, however he destroyed Jerusalem, and ordered dead bodies to be thrown in it, saying: whoever cast a dead body in it, I will reward him. He was assisted by the Romans due to killing John by the Israelites.

After he had destroyed Jerusalem, he took some of the Israelites including Daniel, and when he returned to Babylon, he found Sihaeen has dead, then he became the king, and the Magi said to him: those people you came with, Daniel and his companions, neither they worship you deity, nor they eat from your sacrifice. He then called and asked them, they said: yes, we have God to worship and we can't eat from your sacrifice, then he ordered a trench to be dug for them and they were cast in it and brought a fierce beast to eat them. When they came to them afterwards, they found them sitting and the beast was lying, and they found them seven, they said: you were six, the seventh was a king and he slapped Nebuchadnezzar.

It was reported by Abu Jaafar Altabary: those who held that Nebuchadnezzar is the one who conquered the children of Israel upon killing John are incorrect, since they agreed that Nebuchadnezzar invaded them when they killed their apostle Isaiah at the reign of Armiah, and John was born four hundred and sixty one years before Nebuchadnezzar had destroyed Jerusalem

This is agreed upon between Jews and Christians, and has been recorded in their Scriptures. They held that seventy years separate between the destruction and construction of Jerusalem. They also count eighty-eight years between constructing it and the advent of Alexander who gained control over it. Thus, there has been four hundred and sixty one years between the birth of John and destruction of Jerusalem.

With respect to the Magi: they agree with Jews and Christians regarding the time of Jerusalem destruction. However, they oppose them regarding the time period between the reign of Alexander and the birth of John. They thought that this period is fifty one years.

Mohammed ibn Ishaq said: when the children of Israel came back from Babylon to Jerusalem, they continued in their violations. When apostles were sent to them, they would either deny or kill them. The last of those sent to them were Zechariah, John and Jesus, they were all descendants of David household. When God raised Jesus to Him, and John was killed- and some says that Zechariah also was killed- God has sent upon them a Babylonian king named Khirdos, then he came with the Babylonians until he invaded them in the Levant, he said the chief of his guards: I would swear by my lord: if I seized Jerusalem, I would kill them all until their blood gush out in a military crowd.

When he entered Jerusalem, he found fresh blood boiling, said: what makes this blood boiling? They said: this is a sacrifice we have done and was not accepted. He said: you don't tell me the truth.

He killed a lot of them on this blood until it does calm down. He said: I warn you, I will kill all of you if you don't tell me the truth, hence, they said: this is the blood of the apostle of us, then he said: God took revenge of you for that, he slaughtered horses, cows, mules and sheep until the blood reached Khirdos, then he sent them, saying: enough is that

.

God pointed to this incident in the Quran, saying: "Then when the final promise came, [We sent your enemies] to sadden your faces and to enter the temple in Jerusalem, as they entered it the first time". "فإذا جاء وعد الآخرة ليسئوا وجوهكم وليدخلوا المسجد كما دخلوه أول مرة". (17:7)

The first battle was Nebuchadnezzar and his soldiers, then God gave back to them a return victory over them.

Afterwards, there has been the last battle at the time of Khirdos and his soldiers, which was the greatest of the two incidents, since their men were murdered, their children and wives were captured and their city was destroyed, as God says: "and to destroy what they had taken over with [total]" "وليتبروا ما علوا تتبيرا". (17:7)

Section

God revealed too many apostles between Moses and Jesus, a few of them were mentioned while most of them were not.

Ibn Masoud said: the children of Israel would kill three hundred of apostles per day.

Anas reported the prophet (PBUH) as saying:

"No apostle amongst the apostles has been testified (by such a large number of people) as I have been testified. And verily there would be an apostle among the apostles who would be testified to by only one man from his people."

Among the apostles the companions of the well, Ali ibn Abu Talib said commenting on them: they would worship a tree, then God has sent to them a prophet from the descendants of Judas, son of Jacob, they dug a well for him and cast him in, thus they were destroyed.

Said ibn Jubair said: this prophet was named "Hanzala ibn Safwan", they killed him then God destroyed them.

Qatada and Wahb said: they are the people of Shuaib.

Al Suddy said: he is Habib Al Najjar. And God knows best.

The tale of Jesus, son of Mary (PBUH)

Ibn Abbas reported that:

The time period between Moses, son of Imran; and Jesus (PBUH) is one thousand and seven hundred years, there has been no period of suspension between them. There have been thousands of prophet sent besides those of other nations, the time period that separates between Jesus and Mohammed (PBUH) was five hundred and sixty nine years, starting with three prophets mentioned in the saying of God: "When We sent to them two but they denied them, so We strengthened them with a third, and they said, "Indeed, we are messengers to you'"" إذا أرسلنا إليهم اثنين فكذبوهما "فعززنا بثالث".   (36:14)

The one they were strengthened with was Simeon. The time period during which there was no prophet has been sent was four hundred and eighty years.

The biographers held that: Imran son of Mathan son of Sahim son of 'Amoor son of Meeshan son of Izekiel son of Aharef son of Baoom son of Izarya son of Amsiy son of Nawoos son of Nootha son of Baridh son of Yehushafaz son of Radim son of Abiyya son of Rehobom son of Solomon son of David, has died and his wife- named Hannah was pregnant with Mary, and Zechariah was the husband of Eesha who was Mary's sister. Hannah dedicated what is in her womb freely to the church in the mount of Asbayon. When she delivered her and found out that she was a female, Zechariah took the charge over her. When her mother weaned her, she left her in the Mihrab, and returned to her family, she was provided with the fruits of the Paradise, so Zechariah would find the fruit of the winter there, he would say: O Mary: from where is that? She would reply: it is from God, hence Zechariah made supplication to God to grant him a child.

The tale of Mary's Pregnancy.

When Marry reached the age of fifteen, one day, she had to go out to fetch water from a nearby cave when she suddenly encountered Jibril in human form. He said to her:

"I am only a messenger from your Lord that I may bestow on you a chaste son","إنما أنا رسول ربك لأهب لك غلاما زكيا". (19:19)

The scholars have differed over the period of her pregnancy.

Some say that the duration of her pregnancy was nine months as other women, while others say the pregnancy lasted for eight month, and that was another miracle as no baby who stayed in his mother's womb for just eight months survived except Jesus. Other scholars say it lasted for six months, but others say it was three hours, and some even say it was only one hour.

The tale of what happened to him while she was pregnant

Mujahid has said: Mary(may God be pleased with her) said: "whenever I sought seclusion, Jesus would speak to me, and I would speak to him. If a human distracted me from that, he would praise the Almighty while being in my womb, and I would hear his praising,".

The tale of Jesus birth

Noof al Bikaly said: she run away from her family to an eastern place, they went out asking about her. Whenever they met anyone they would say: did you see a girl like that? They would say: No.

They finally met across a cow shepherd, they asked him, he said : no, but I saw something weird of my cows that they prostrated toward this valley.

God said: "And the pains of childbirth drove her to the trunk of a palm tree. She said, Oh, I wish I had died before this and was in oblivion, forgotten." " فجاءها المخاض إلى جذع النخلة قالت يا ليتني مت قبل هذا وكنت نسيا منسيا"" (19:23)

Jibril called her: don't be sad, so she delivered Jesus and wrapped him in a rag and cut his belly button.

Wahab said: "when Jesus was born, all idols were falling on the ground in each and every land, so that the devils were terrified and did not know the reason behind such matter. They rushed to Satan the damned, complaining to him.

Instantaneously, Satan flew away for three hours during which he by-passed the place where Jesus was born, he was surrounded by the angels around him from every direction, so Satan can't approach Jesus. God the Almighty safeguarded, his profit Jesus.

This is confirmed by the Prophet's saying, Abu Huraira quoted the Messenger as saying:

No child is born but he is pricked by Satan and he begins to weep because of the pricking of Satan except the son of Mary and his mother.

Abu Huraira then said: You may recite if you so like (the verse):"I seek Thy protection for her and her offspring against Satan the accursed". " "وإني أعيذها بك وذريتها من الشيطان الرجيم" (19:36).

The tale of what happened with her when her people met her

When Mary came to her family with the infant, they said to her:

"O Mary, you have certainly done a thing unprecedented", "قالوا يا مريم لقد جئت شيئا فريا"

(19:28), whereupon, she pointed to him. They said, "How can we speak to one who is in the cradle a child?", "فأشارت إليه قالوا كيف we speak نكلم من كان في المهد صبيا"(19:29).

[Jesus] said, "Indeed, I am the servant of God . He has given me the Scripture and made me a prophet", قال إني عبد الله آتاني الكتاب "وجعلني نبيا"". (19:30)

The tale of description of Jesus [PBUH]

Abu Huraira reported that the Messenger said:

I am most close to Jesus, son of Mary, among the whole of mankind in this worldly life and the next life. People asked: God's Messenger how is it? Thereupon he said: prophets are brothers in faith, having different mothers. Their religion is, however, one and there is no Apostle between us (between I and Jesus Christ).

The tale of his dwelling [PBUH]

Jesus (PBUH) was settling in Khalil in a town called Nazareth in Arabic name al- Nasira.

The tale of what happened to him while he was in the class

Said ibn Jubair said: when Jesus matured, his mother took him to the class and seated him before the teacher. The teacher asked Jesus to say In name of , then Jesus said: God, then the teacher said: most Gracious, then Jesus said: most Merciful. Whereupon the teacher said: how can I teach who knows more than me. He used to tell his fellow what their parents were doing and what they have eaten such-and-such food.

The tale of his prophethood and his miracles

The biographers stated: at the age of thirty, Allah inspired Jesus to come out to the public, to invite them to worship the One and Only God. Then, Jesus came to Jerusalem, he was empowered by the will of God to heal the sick, to cure those suffering permanent handicaps, to give sight back to the born blind and heal the leprous. The reason these two diseases were mainly mentioned is attributing to the fact that no physician of that time could discover any cure for them. Jesus lived during a time when medicine was considered the most notorious branch of knowledge, so he was able to show to the people miracles in it, which nobody else could.

Besides, he was empowered to heal the mentally retarded, and make a bird out of a clay by the permission of God, and he would inform them what they have eaten in their homes, his book was the Bible, his nourishment was the Torah and he was knowledgeable of Zabur (the holy book of David)

Among his signs was the banquet and walking on the water. Besides, he was praising Godin the womb of his mother. He was talking, while he was in the cradle

Wahab has said: fifty thousand of sick people were come at the door of his house.

Salman Alfarisy said: all the sick or the afflicted with ailment would gather at him and he would invoke to God for them, so they were cured by the permission of God, whereupon they believed in him, then they said to him: bring life back to a dead person, he said: who do you want? They said: Sam, son Of Noah, he has died many thousands years ago, he said: you know where his grave is? They said: in the place of such and such.

He said: let's go to the valley, then he performed two prostrations, then he said: O' my God, they asked me what you know so bring life back to Sam, son of Noah. He (Jesus) said: O' Sam, son of Noah, come back to life by the will of God, then he called him second, then he called him third, then the earth split and Sam came out of his grave, saying: I am responding to you and I am at your service. He said: O' children of Israel, this is Jesus son of the blessed virgin Mary, so believe in him and follow him.

Then he said: O' spirit of God, when you call me first, God gathered my bones and muscles, and when you called me second, God brought my life back to me, and when you called me third I feared that this would be the Doomsday, so my hair became gray and an angel came to me, saying: this is Jesus calling you to believe in him. O' Jesus! ask your Lord to bring me back to the Afterlife, I have nothing to do with the worldly life.

Jesus said: would you like to be with me, then he replied: O' Jesus, I hate the agony of death, so he prayed his Lord and God put him to death, whereupon the number of those who believed in Jesus has reached seven thousand people.

Inspirations by God to Jesus

God inspired Jesus: remember me in this worldly life, and I will remember you in the Afterlife, stay up at night and keep reciting the Bible. Be humble whenever My Name is mentioned, submissive with heart whenever you yourself mention Me, awake when the heedless sleep. When you enter a mosque of Mine, let your heart be humble of fear from Me, and your organs be humbled before Me. Inform your people, when you come to a mosque of Mine, Have your hearts fear of Me, and your eyes be humbled before Me, and purify your hands from evil doing. And inform them that I don't answer the supplication of an oppressor until he give back the right to the oppressed. O' Jesus, do not sit with the one who errs constantly until he repents. O' Jesus, I remember whoever remembers Me, and I curse the oppressor.

The tale of the life and asceticism of Prophet Jesus (PBUH)

Salman Al Farisi "the Persian" said: Jesus (PBUH) used to wear a woolen garment during the day and a camel's hair garment during the night. Further, he never laughed in a loud manner.

Mujahid said: Jesus (PBUH) had no son that may die, no wife or a house that may be destroyed. Once bedtime rolled around, he slept wherever he was. Further, he did not save anything for the future.

It was narrated by some people of the Scripture who then embraced Islam that: Jesus (PBUH) was touring the globe; he did not settle in a certain dwelling or a certain village. He used to wear a hooded cloak and a lower garment which were made of camel's hair. He was wearing tanned leather sandals and holding a walking stick. He lodged where the night grew dark over him. He considered the darkness of night as his shade. He simply laid out on the floor and his pillow was such a stone. His food was the green herbs and he might spend days hungry. He did not feel sorrow in hard times nor he felt boastful in good times.

It was reported by Al Hasan that: Once a day, Satan passed by Prophet Jesus (PBUH) while he was resting his head on a stone. Satan said to him: "O' Jesus, do not you claim that you have no desire for the short term pleasures of this worldly life?". So, Prophet Jesus (PBUH) stood, carried the stone and threw it on Satan and said to him: "This is for you along with the worldly life".

It was reported that Imran ibn Muslim said:

I was informed that Prophet Jesus, the son of Mary, (PBUH) went out to his companions, wearing a woolen cloak, woolen garment and underpants, having his hair and moustache cut, inclined to cry, appearing pale because of hunger, suffering dry lips because of thirst and having a long hair in his chest, arms and legs. Then, he said: "Peace be upon you. O' the descendants of Israel, neglect the worldly life in order that it will be easy for you. Degrade the worldly life so that you will attain your desires in the Afterlife. Do not degrade the Afterlife in order not to be degraded in the worldly life; because the worldly life is not an abode of sublimity. It calls every day for temptation and loss".

Then, he said to his companions: "Do you know where is my house?". They said: "Where is it, O' the spirit created by the command of God?". So, he said: "My dwelling is the mosques, my perfume is water, my condiment is hunger, my means of transportation is my legs, my illuminating lamp in the night is the moon, my shade is the dark night and my dwelling in winter is wherever the sun rises, my food is the dried one, my fruit is green herbs, my garment is that made of wool, my motto is fearing God and my companions are the weak and needy. The morning and the evening pass and I possess nothing for myself, but being of good cheer and do not care about the ones who are richer than me".

It was narrated by Mohammed ibn shujaa Al Numairy that:

While Jesus, the son of Mary, was going around somewhere in the Levant, it rained heavily and there were thunder and lightning. So, he began to look for some place to take a refuge. Then, he saw a tent at a far distance. However, when he approached it, he found a woman there, so, he turned away from it. Afterwards, he saw a cave in a mountain. Unfortunately, when he reached it, he found a lion there. So, he raised his hands to supplicate God and said: "My Lord, You have made a refuge for every living creature except for me". So, God, the Majestic, Almighty and Sublime, responded to his supplication by revealing to him: "Your refuge is in the settlement of My mercy. On the Doomsday, I will marry you to one hundred fair women whom I have formed with My hand. And I will set for your wedding feast enough food to eat for four hundred years, each day of which will be of the length of this worldly life. And I will order a herald to announce: 'Where are the abstemious who abstain from the things of the worldly life? Come and attend the wedding feast of the abstemious Jesus, the son of Mary'". Yet, this is HADITH DAIF (WEAK).

The tale of some admonitions of Jesus (PBUH)

It was reported by Wahb ibn Munabbih that Jesus, the son of Mary, said:

"Wisdom has its own people who are worthy of it. If you keep it from the worthy, you will be unjust. And if you expose wisdom before the unworthy, you will be ignorant. So, be like an expert doctor who applies medicine to the place of sickness".

It was reported by some people of the Scripture who then embraced Islam that Jesus (PBUH) admonished the disciples:

"Do not accompany the ones who constantly commit sins, because accompanying them will make you harsh-hearted. Draw closer to God, the Almighty and Sublime, by deserting them. O' assembly of the disciples, do not worry for tomorrow, rather, only consider the current day. Also, do not worry for the provision of tomorrow, for the Creator of tomorrow will give you provision therein. If winter comes, none of you shall say: 'By which means can I eat or wear?'. And if summer comes, none of you shall say: 'By which means can I eat or drink?'. If you are kept alive in winter, you will be given provision. Similarly, if you are kept alive in summer, you will be given provision. Do not worry about winter and summer during your current day. Rather, take each day as it comes.

O' assembly of the disciples, a descendant of Adam is created in the worldly life in four positions. He trusts God and thinks good of Him in three positions. However, in the fourth position, he does not have firm faith in his Lord.

As for the first position, a descendant of Adam is created in the womb of his mother, in one stage after another, within three veils of darkness: the darkness of the womb, the darkness of the uterus, and the darkness of the placenta. While he is in the darkness of the womb, God gives him provision. When he comes out of the womb, he is fed breast milk without exerting any effort; he does not walk to get it or drink it with his hand. Rather, he is forced to suck it, until he gets weaned. Then, he reaches the third position in which he is being raised by his two kind parents. If they die and let him be an orphan, people will be kind towards him; someone will feed him, another one will cloth him as a way of being merciful towards him. When he reaches the fourth position, where his shape becomes in due proportion – becomes an adult - and none will give him provision except God, he begins to challenge God and engage in conflict with people for possessing the worldly life.

O' assembly of the disciples, learn a lesson from birds. Have you ever seen a bird that reserves things for the future? Of course not, so do the beasts and voracious animals. I speak the truth to you, you become in a time of people whose words are like that of the prophets while whose deeds are as that of the fools. Their words are like medicine that heals disease but your hearts do not respond to medicine. Your hearts cry because of your bad deeds. For you, the worldly life becomes as if it were a beautiful bride adored by whosoever sees her, whereas she is like a snake whose touch is tender but whose poison causes murder.

O' assembly of the disciples, focus your concern amongst the worldly life on yourselves so that God becomes pleased with you. Do not focus your concern on your carnal lusts and excessive appetite for food, considering that as a matter of wisdom, rather you can eat barley bread and crushed salt; for well-being in this worldly life and the Afterlife. Bear in mind that gazing at women is a temptation by Satan and generates carnal lust in the heart. A wise person who says and acts wisely is like the sun that illuminates for creatures and does not burn itself. On the other hand, a wise person who does not act wisely is like a lamp that illuminates the place around and burns itself.

O' assembly of the disciples, do not focus on the sins of people as if you were lords. Instead, focus on your sins as you are not but slaves to your Only Lord. There are two kinds of people: some are afflicted with sins and some are protected from committing sins. So, be merciful to the people of affliction and praise God for His protection.

O' descendants of Israel, forgive people so that you will be forgiven by God, the Almighty and Sublime. Do not speak wisely to people while your hearts are bearing rancor towards them. Glad tidings is to those who are devoutly supplicating God during the night.

O' those who are keen on the worldly life, you will not get what you aspire to unless you are patient, endure misfortunes and what you do not like and control your desires. You were lifeless and God brought life to you. Then, your hearts died, i.e. became harsh. When you were astray, God guided you. Then, you got astray again. Know that the female fornicator gets divulged if she becomes pregnant. Similarly, the one who deceives people with good words while he does not do the things he says will be divulged by his deed.

The tale of the events that happened in the era of Jesus (PBUH)

The belief of the disciples in Jesus (PBUH):

They were twelve men who followed Prophet Jesus (PBUH). It was said that they were the ones who asked Prophet Jesus (PBUH) to supplicate God for sending down to them a table set with viands from heaven.

Jesus dispatched two men of the disciples to Antakya to admonish its people to believe in God:

It was reported by Qatada with regard to God's saying: "And present to them an example: the people of the city, when the messengers came to it" "وَاضْرِبْ لَهُم مَّثَلًا أَصْحَابَ الْقَرْيَةِ إِذْ جَاءَهَا الْمُرْسَلُونَ" (36:13), that it was mentioned that those messengers referred to in this verse were two men of the disciples sent by Prophet Jesus (PBUH), the son of Mary, to Antakya (a Roman city). They were denied so Jesus (PBUH) sent a third messenger there. This meaning was also referred to by Ibn Juraij. On the other hand, some scholars, amongst which were Kaab and Wahb, said that God, Exalted is He, was the one who sent those messengers. However, it may be interpreted that they were sent by God even though Prophet Jesus (PBUH) sent them; because they were the messengers of God's Messenger, Jesus (PBUH).

The scholars differed regarding the names of the two messengers. There were three sayings: Firstly: Sadik and Masdouk, said by ibn Abbas and Kaab. Secondly: John and Jonah, said by Wahb. Thirdly: Umar and Paul, said by Muqatil. And he said that the third messenger was called Simon who was one of the disciples and the tutor succeeding Jesus (PBUH).

Kaab said: When God, the Almighty and Sublime, sent the messengers to Antakya because its people were worshipping idols, they were denied and threatened of being murdered. So, Habib Al Najjar came to advise people to obey the messengers. God Says in the Holy Quran: "O my people, follow the messengers". "قَالَ يَا قَوْم اتَّبِعُوا الْمُرْسَلِينَ" (36:20). Consequently, they killed him.

Ibn Masoud said: They kicked him till he died. When he moved into God's mercy, he said, as mentioned in the Holy Quran: "I wish my people could know, Of how my Lord has forgiven me and placed me among the honored" " بِمَا. يَعْلَمُونَ قَوْمِي لَيْتَ يَا (36:27), (غَفَرَ لِي رَبِّي وَجَعَلَنِي مِنَ الْمُكْرَمِينَ" (36:26). God became angry with them because they reckoned him as naught and killed him. Therefore, God hastened the punishment for them. He sent down to them a gale-force blast, so, they fell down lifeless.

The meeting of Jesus (PBUH) with Satan (cursed by God):

Abu Al Jalad said: Jesus, the son of Mary, met Satan. So, he told him: "I ask you, by the Ever-Living, the Sustainer of all existence Who has cursed you, what does cripple you and what destroys your body?". Satan fell himself to the ground, then he rose and said: "I would not inform you unless you asked me by the Ever-Living, the Sustainer of all existence. As for the thing that cripples me, it is Man's performance of supergeratory (Nawafil) prayers at home and obligatory prayers at masjid. As for the thing that destroys my body, it is the whinnying of horses in the cause of God, the Almighty and Sublime, i.e. holy struggle in the cause of God (jihad)".

The murder of John, the son of Zechariah

John (PBUH) was killed during the era of Jesus (PBUH).

Among the events occurred during the era of Jesus (PBUH) was the soil infertility and his prayer for rain

It was reported by ibn Abbas that:

Jesus, the son of Mary, went forth with people to ask God for rain. Then, God, the Almighty and Sublime, revealed to him: "Let the one who has constantly committed sins go". So, Jesus (PBUH) said to them: "The sinners should turn away from us". So, they all turned away except one man whose right eye was gouged out. Then, Jesus said to him: "Why do not you turn away?". The man replied to him: "O' the spirit created by the command of God, I did not disobey God for a glance, except that once a day I unintentionally looked at the foot of a woman with this eye. So, I plucked it out. Besides, if I were to look at her with my left eye, I would pluck it out also".

Thereupon, Jesus (PBUH) cried for him till his beard got wet. Then, Jesus said to him: "You have to pray to God for rain. I am protected by the revelation but you are not and you did not commit a sin for you had looked at the woman unintentionally". So, the man raised his hands for supplicating God. Accordingly, by the one in whose Hand is the soul of Jesus, immediately after he finished supplication, it rained heavily and the town dweller as well as the visitor drank.

Among the events occurred during the era of Jesus (PBUH) was the descending of the table from heaven:

It was reported by Salman Al Farisi that:

When the disciples asked Jesus (PBUH) to supplicate God, Exalted is He, for sending down to them a table set with viands from the heaven, Jesus (PBUH) humbly kept his head down and prayed to God, saying: "O Allah, our Lord, send down to us a table [spread with food] from the heaven to be for us a festival for the first of us and the last of us" " اللَّـهُمَّ رَبَّنَا أنزِلْ عَلَيْنَا مَائِدَةً مِّنَ السَّمَاءِ تَكُونُ لَنَا عِيدًا لِّأَوَّلِنَا وَآخِرِنَا" (5:114)". And he continued his supplication by saying: "so that Your provision for us will be a sign from You".

Afterwards, a red dining table descended between two clouds, falling in the air at their sight. Prophet Jesus (PBUH) cried out of fearing God and said: "O' my God, let this table be a mercy, not a punishment", until it settled before Prophet Jesus. The people around him found the best smell they have ever had. So, Jesus (PBUH) bowed down in prostration to God, the Almighty and Sublime, and the disciples did as well. Hence, this news reached the Jews. So, they came to Jesus and his companions. They saw an eccentric matter; a dining table covered with a cloth. Then, Jesus (PBUH) said: "Which of us is the most faithful and truthful with his Lord in order to uncover this sign so that we shall look at it and eat from it?". The disciples said: "O' the spirit created by the command of God and His word, you are the most worthy of it".

Consequently, Prophet Jesus (PBUH) made the ablution again and supplicated his Lord a lot, crying. Then, he rose up and sat at the dining table. There appeared a thornless fish having vinegar placed at its head and salt at its tail, and five loaves of bread on every one of which there were olives and five pomegranates, and round the fish were all sorts of herbs. Simon, the head of the disciples, said: "O' the spirit created by the command of God, does this provision belong to the food of the worldly life or that of the Heaven?". Jesus (PBUH) said: "Glory be to God, will you not stop that? I fear for you to be punished by God". Simon said: "By God, the Lord of the descendants of Israel, I do not intend something ill by saying so". Jesus (PBUH) said: "This food you see does not belong to the worldly life nor to the Afterlife. Rather, it is created by the mighty of God, the Almighty and Sublime. He only said to it: "Be" and it was. So, eat what you have asked for and praise your Lord for it".

They said: "O' the spirit created by the command of God, shall you show us a miracle with this fish?". Jesus (PBUH) said to the fish: "Come back to life by the permission of God, Exalted is He". So, it was restored to life. Then, he said to it: "Return to your previous state by the permission of God". So, it became as it was before, ready to be eaten.

Jesus (PBUH) called the people afflicted with poverty, bodily infirmities, the blind, leprous, disabled and so on. He said to them: "Eat from the provision given by God Who responded to the supplication of your Prophet. This will be a bless for you and a trial and a punishment for the deniers".

One thousand and three hundred men and women ate from these provisions and were satisfied. The food on the table remained whole as it was at first upon its descending. Then, the table flew up to heaven at the sight of all people. Everyone who had partaken of this food, were delivered from their infirmities and misfortunes. Everyone who refused to eat from the table felt remorse. Therefore, when it descended afterwards, they all came to it from here and there; the rich and the poor, men and women, the sick and healthy. So, Jesus made them eat from it in turn.

The table continued to descend for forty days. Then, God revealed to Jesus (PBUH): "Let My table be a provision only for the orphans and infirm, not the rich ones". As a result, the rich became so enraged. Thus, they tried to make the people disbelieve in this miracle and they themselves suspected it to the extent that one of them said to Jesus (PBUH): "O' the spirit created by the command of God, is this table truthfully descended by God?". Jesus (PBUH) said: "Woe to you, you will be punished if God, Exalted is He, does not have mercy upon you". Thereupon, God, Exalted is He, revealed to Jesus, the son of Mary, (PBUH) that He will punish the deniers as He has previously imposed a condition of punishment on whosoever disbelieves after getting the request of the miraculous table. God says: "Indeed, I will sent it down to you, but whoever disbelieves afterwards from among you - then indeed will I punish him with a punishment by which I have not punished anyone among the worlds" " إِنِّي مُنَزِّلُهَا عَلَيْكُمْ فَمَن يَكْفُرْ بَعْدُ مِنكُمْ فَإِنِّي أُعَذِّبُهُ عَذَابًا لَّا أُعَذِّبُهُ أَحَدًا مِّنَ الْعَالَمِينَ" (5:115)".

The reason for the ascension of Jesus (PBUH) into heaven

Wahb ibn Munabbih said: Jesus (PBUH) was accompanied by seventeen men among the disciples when the disbelievers came to kill him. So, Jesus (PBUH) said: "Which one of you can dispense with his soul in return for the Heaven?". One of them agreed. So, the disbelievers crucified and killed this man because he was made to look like Jesus before them. And Jesus (PBUH) was raised to God. Some scholars said: this man was called Joshua.

Said ibn Al Musayyab said: God raised Jesus (PBUH) to Him while he was thirty three years old. It was said that God, the

Almighty and Sublime, sent revelation to Prophet Jesus after he had reached the age of thirty. The revelation continued for three years. Then, it was ceased after his ascending to heaven. So, there was a period of cessation of revelation to a prophet till Prophet Mohammed (PBUH) was sent.

However, it was said: there were four messengers who were sent during the period between Jesus (PBUH) and Mohammed (PBUH), three of which are mentioned in the Holy Quran. God says: "When We sent to them two but they denied them, so We strengthened them with a third, and they said, "Indeed, we are messengers to you" " إِذْ أَرْسَلْنَا إِلَيْهِمُ اثْنَيْنِ فَكَذَّبُوهُمَا فَعَزَّزْنَا بِثَالِثٍ فَقَالُوا إِنَّا إِلَيْكُم "مُّرْسَلُونَ (36:14)". The fourth messenger was Khalid ibn Sinan Al Absi. Yet, it was reported by Prophet Mohammed (PBUH) that he said about Prophet Jesus (PBUH): "There has been no prophet between me and him". So, what about the four messengers? Some may interpret that by saying that no prophet calls for a new religion, rather, he calls for the same religion of the prophet preceding him in which people already believed. A prophet reminds people of being pious; do good deeds and avoid evil ones. All prophets embrace only one religion that is of monotheism, which is Islam. The ordained ways of worship are the ones that may be different from one prophet to the other. And God Knows best. As for the four messengers who were sent in the period between Prophet Jesus and Prophet Jesus, they were sent to the disbeliever people. So, they called them to monotheism. Historians said: There was a period of five thousand five hundred and thirty two years between the descending of Adam (PBUH) to the earth and the ascending of the Messiah, Jesus (PBUH), to the heaven.

The tale of the state of Jesus (PBUH) upon his descending from the heaven

It was narrated by Abu Hurayrah that Prophet Mohammed (PBUH) said about Prophet Jesus (PBUH): "He will descend to the earth to break the cross, kill swine and abolish jizyah, i.e. a poll tax. There will be abundant wealth. During his time period, God will perish all religions except Islam and God will destroy the Antichrist, i.e. the false Messiah (AdDajjal) by the hand of Jesus (PBUH). The whole earth will be safe to the extent that the predators such as lions, tigers and wolves will be grazed with domestic animals such as camels, cows and sheep. Boys will play with snakes without being harmed. Jesus (PBUH) will live on the earth for forty years. Then, he will die and the Muslims will pray over him".

It was reported by Al Nawwas ibn Simaan that Prophet Mohammed (PBUH) said: "Jesus (PBUH) will descend at the white minaret to the east of Damascus".

It was claimed that Abdullah ibn Umar reported that the Messenger of God, Mohammed (PBUH), said: "Prophet Jesus, the son of Mary, (Peace be upon them all) will descend to the earth and marry, have an offspring, live for forty five years and be buried beside his grave". Yet, this is HADITH DAIF.

The tale of the events occurred immediately after the ascension of Jesus (PBUH)

Division of creeds:

It was narrated by Qatada that: It was mentioned that when Jesus (PBUH) was ascended to heaven, four scholars were chosen among the descendants of Israel to be asked about Jesus (PBUH). The people said to the first scholar: "What do you think about Jesus?". He said: "He is God, who descended to the earth, created whatever he willed and brought life back to whichever he willed. Then, he ascended to heaven". So, some people followed him and the Jacobite Christian sect generated accordingly.

However, the three other scholars said to him: "We certify that you are false". So, the people said to the second one: "What do you think about Jesus?". He said: "He is the son of God". Some people followed him. So, the Nestorian Christian sect generated. Yet, the two other scholars said to him: "We certify that you are false". Therefore, the people repeated the same question over the third one. So, he said: "He is a deity and his mother is so and God is a deity. Consequently, some people pledged allegiance to him and the Israelite Christian sect generated and was called the king religion. Hence, the fourth scholar said: "I certify that you are false. Jesus is a Messenger of God, His word which He directed to Mary and a spirit created by His command". As a result, the people disputed with each other. So, the Muslim man said: "I adjure you by God, do you know that Jesus was eating?". They said: "Yes". He said: "Do you know that God does not eat?". They said: "By God, yes". He said: "Then, I adjure you by God, do you know that Jesus was sleeping?". They said: "Yes". He said: "Do you know that God, the Almighty and Sublime, does not sleep?". They said: "Yes". So, he confuted them with reason, articulating the matter for them in a more convincing way.

Among the events occurred after the ascension of Jesus, the son of Mary (Peace be upon them all), was the death of Mary:

Mary lived for six years after the ascension of Jesus (PBUH) to heaven. Her age was little more than fifty years.

The tale of the events of the war occurred among the disciples after the ascension of Jesus (PBUH) to heaven

Ibn Isaac said: When the Jews intended to kill Jesus (PBUH) and they crucified the one who appeared to be like him before their eyes, they aggressed against the disciples and seized them. The Roman king heard about that news, and he was an idol worshipper. He was told by some people (as they falsely thought that Jesus (PBUH) was the one who was murdered): "Those people among the descendants of Israel who are under your rule murdered a man, even though he informed them that he was the messenger of God and showed them miracles; he brought the dead forth to life again, healed the sick and told them about the hidden". The king said: "Woe to you, why did not you tell me about that news so that I would protect him". Hence, he sent messengers to free the disciples and bring them to him. He asked them about the religion of Jesus (PBUH) and they answered him. So, he pledged allegiance to them that he would embrace their religion. Thereupon, Christianity originally generated in Rome.

Wahb ibn Munabbih said: The disciples assembled after the ascension of Jesus (PBUH) to heaven. They said: "We wish to go forth to call people to worship God". Among the ones who went to Rome were Nestorius and his two companions. Nestorius instructed them to gently advise people to be pious. However, his two companions did not obey him. They were tough advisors. So, they were seized by the command of the king. When the people were confused between the lawful and the unlawful, they used to raise the argument to the king. So, he discussed the matter with the people. Once a time, Nestorius was present among them and replied well to the matter of argument. The king admired Nestorius, honored him by letting him dwell near his throne. Further, Nestorius used to interpret for the king anything he asked about. Then, Nestorius along with his two companions tried to gently convince the king and his people that the idols which they considered as deities could not harm nor benefit. So, Nestorius said to the king to ask the deities to harm these two men; his two companions. Of course, the deities did not react at all. So, Nestorius told the king that his two companions had the capability of destroying these deities. So, the king gave the permission to do. And they demolished them. Consequently, Nestorius said: "As for me, I believe in the Lord of these two men". The king also said so. In addition, all people said like that. Then, Nestorius said to his two companions: "Gentleness can do".

The tale of the kings who came after Jesus (PBUH)

The tale of what regards to the Greek and the people of the Levant

It was said that the Jews believed in the Messiah, Jesus (PBUH), during the reign of Caesar Herod over Jerusalem. After his death, his son Archelaus, succeeded him. After his death, Herod □□ succeeded him. During his reign, the man who was made to appear like Jesus (PBUH) at the sight of the Jews was crucified. Caesar was the title of the Great kings who ruled the Roman state. The judge at the time of Herod □□ was a Roman man called Pilatus who was assigned by Caesar. Tiberius ibn Augustus ruled for twenty three years. Among this ruling period were eighteen years and few days before the ascension of Jesus (PBUH), the Messiah, to heaven, whereas he ruled for five years after the ascension of Jesus (PBUH). After the death of Tiberius, came the reign of his son, Gaius, over the Levant, which continued for four years. Then, came the reign of his other son who was called Claudius, which continued for fourteen years. Then, he was succeeded by Nero who killed Peter and Paul, and ruled for fourteen years. Then, came the reign of Vespasian, which continued for ten years. After the first three years of his reign and forty years following the ascension of Jesus (PBUH) to heaven, Vespasian dispatched his son, Titus, to Jerusalem to destroy it and kill many people belonging to the descendants of Israel to take revenge for the murder of Jesus (PBUH), the Messiah (as they falsely thought that he had been murdered). Afterwards, Titus succeeded his father for two years. Then, he was succeeded by Domitian for sixteen years. Then, he was succeeded by Trajan for nineteen years. Then, he was succeeded by Hadrian for twenty one years. Then, he was succeeded by Titus, the son of Pius, for twenty two years. Then, he was succeeded by Marcus and his son for nineteen years. Then, Commodus ruled for thirteen years. Then, he was succeeded by Pertinax for six months. Then, he was succeeded by Severus for fourteen years. Then, he was succeeded by Antonius for four years. Then, he was succeeded by Marcian for six years. Then, he was succeeded by Elagabalus for four years. Then, Alexander ruled for thirteen years. Afterwards, came to the reign forty men one at a time. Their names are like those ones. So, there is no need to mention them to be brief.

After the end of the reign of the forty men, Heraclius came to the reign for thirty years, to whom the Messenger of God, Mohammed (PBUH) sent letters. There was a period of little more than one thousand years between the time of reconstructing Jerusalem after it had been destroyed by Nebuchadnezzar and the time of the migration (Hijrah) of our Prophet, Mohammed (PBUH).

The time period between the reign of the Greek Alexander and the migration of Prophet Mohammed (PBUH) was little more than nine hundred and twenty years, of which were three hundred and three years before the birth of Prophet Jesus (PBUH). The time period between his birth and the time of his ascension to heaven was thirty three years. The time period between the ascension of Jesus (PBUH) to heaven and the migration of Prophet Mohammed (PBUH) was five hundred eighty five years and few months. The murder of Prophet John, the son of Prophet Zechariah, occurred after the first eight years of the reign of Ardashir ibn Babak (Ardashir I).

The tale of the events regarding the Arabs

It was said that after the death of Nebuchadnezzar, the Arabs who had dwelled in the city of Al Hirah joined the people of Al Anbar governorate. So, the city of Al Hirah became ruined for a long period of time; nobody of the Arabs inhabited there whereas Al Anbar was inhabited by its people along with the people who joined them from among Al Hirah and the descendants of Ishmael and Maad ibn Adnan from among the Arab tribes. They grew in number in Tihama and beyond. Then, a war broke out among them. So, they went forth seeking the countryside which was at Yemen and the states of Al Mashriq (in another narration, the Levant). Some of them dwelled in Bahrain where there was the tribe of Al Azd. This tribe had dwelled there in the era of Imran ibn Amr.

Some of the Arab tribes assembled in Bahrain and formed an alliance to support and advocate each other. Then, they were called the Tanukhids or Tanukh (which is an Arabic term means a confederation). Malik ibn Zuhayr married Jadhima ibn Al Abrash ibn Malik ibn Fahm to his sister, Lumays, the daughter of Zuhayr. All of these events took place during the time period of the kings of factions (known in Arabic as Muluk Al Tawaif) who were assigned by Alexander. They were so called because he divided the state among them into small kingdoms after he had murdered Dara ibn Dara (Darius II) – the king of Persia – till Ardashir ibn Babak became the king of Persia over the kings of factions and conquered them.

Then, the Arabs who were in Bahrain aspired to the countryside in Iraq. They wanted to take over or share the regions dominated by the Ajam - i.e. non Arabs – beyond the Arab states. So, they were divided into many chiefs, every one of which went forth along with his allies to invade a nation. They still engaged in war till Tubba – who was also called Asaad Abu Karib ibn MalikiKarib – came at the head of his armies. The ones who had no power to fight did not accompany him. And he went forth for raiding.

Many of the Tanukhids from Al Anbar and Al Hirah dwelled in the west of the Euphrates river in tents rather than in clay buildings. The first king in the time period of the kings of factions was Malik ibn Fahm. He dwelled beyond Al Anbar governorate. After the death of Malik, his brother, Amr ibn Fahm, succeeded him. Then he died and was succeeded by Jadhima ibn Al Abrash ibn Malik ibn Fahm ibn Daws Al Azdi. He was one of the best Arab kings, who excelled them in thought, defiance and insight. He was the first king over Iraq and the Arabs joined him. He was leprous – which is spelled "Abras" in Arabic - but the Arabs did not call him so; because they honored him, and called him Jadhima Al Abrash instead. He invaded the land located between Al Hirah, Al Anbar, Baqqa, Hit and its district, and Ayn Al Tamr, and its desert range. Taxes were collected to him and delegations used to come to him. He went forth to raid the tribes of Tasm and Jadis but he found that Hassan ibn Tubba preceded him there. So, he turned back along with his companions. Amongst those tribes was the woman called Zarqaa Al Yamama. Her country was named after her Al Yamama. She was one of the daughters of Luqman ibn Aad. It was said that she belonged to the tribes of Jadis and Tasm.

When the army of Hassan ibn Tubba pursued Jadhima and his companions, it was at a distance, valued by marching for three days, far from them. However, Zarqaa Al Yamama saw the army of Hassan and every soldier of his army was carrying a tree. She alerted her tribe saying: "I swear by God, the trees are moving towards us, behind which soldiers hide" – or "the Himyarite troops are coming". Unfortunately, her tribe did not believe her. So, she repeated her warning once more but in vain. The troops of Hassan eventually reached them, conquered them and tore out Zarqaa's eyes.

Then, Adi ibn Nasr ibn Rabiaa married Raqash bint Malik – the sister of Jadhima. Then, Adi ibn Nasr was killed while his wife Raqash was pregnant. She gave birth to a male baby whom she called Amr. His maternal uncle, Jadhima, admired and loved him. Then, Amr got disappeared for a long period of time. Two brothers who were called Malik and Uqail came from the tribe of Al Qayn pursuing Jadhima and bringing gifts for him. While they were eating, a boy seeming pale with a displeased appearance came to them and asked them for food. So, they gave him what he needed. Then, Malik and Uqail asked him: "Who are you?".

He said: "I am Amr ibn Adi". So, they hugged him, got him in a better appearance. Then, they said: "There is no gift that is more precious to give to Jadhima than his sister's son, Amr". Consequently, they accompanied him to Jadhima in Al Hirah. The latter became so happy accordingly and he sent him to his mother. Amr stayed with her for some days. Then, she sent him back to her brother as he ardently loved him. Afterwards, Jadhima said to Malik and Uqail to ask for whatever they wished. They asked him to be his intimate companions forever. And he agreed.

At that time, the king of the Arabs who was ruling Al Hirah (as it was said) and the suburbs of the Levant was Amr ibn Zarib – and it was said: Dharif – ibn Hassan ibn Udhayna ibn Al Sumaidaa ibn Hubar Al Amlaqi – he was also called Al Amliqi. Jadhima mobilized his troops of the Arabs and directed to raid him. When they met, a heavy fighting erupted between both parties. As a result, Amr ibn Dharif was killed and his troops fled. Jadhima turned back with his companions safe and sound. Then, his daughter, Al Zabba, named Nailah (Zenobia), succeeded him. Her troops were the remnants of the Amalekites and those who joined them from the tribes of Qudaa. Al Zabba had a sister called Zabibah for whom she built a well-fortified palace along the western bank of the Euphrates. She used to spend the winter with her sister and the spring at Batn Al Najjar from where she would go to Palmyra (Tadmur).

When her power got well established and she became well entrenched in her reign, she decided to attack Jadhima Al Abrash to avenge the death of her father. However, her sister, Zabibah, who was thoughtful and clever, said to her: "O' Al Zabba, if you raid Jadhima, surely there will be consequences. If you triumph over him, you will have taken your revenge; but if you are murdered, your kingdom will be lost. War is a matter of ups and downs and its pitfalls cannot be avoided. Your glory still prevails over your opponents and contestants. You have not yet encountered trouble or changes of fate. You cannot be sure who may be the triumphant and upon whom the turn of misfortune may befall!". Al Zabba said to her: "You are sensible and offer good advice that I will follow".

She gave up the idea of raiding Jadhima and tended to follow the way of trickery and deception instead in order to fulfill her strategy. In this regard, she sent a letter to Jadhima to call him to marry her and join his kingdom to hers. She justified her demand by saying that she found that the reign of women was weak and she considered nobody efficient for ruling her kingdom and worthy for her other than him. When the letter of Al Zabba reached Jadhima, he became greedy of her offer. He sought the opinion of his sensible companions whom he trusted. At that time, he was at Al Baqqa on the bank of the Euphrates. They agreed that he should proceed to her and take over her kingdom. However, among them there was a man, who was an influential advisor to Jadhima, objected to their opinion and thought that this offer would be a treachery. This man was called Qasir ibn Saad ibn Amr. His mother was a maid for Jadhima. He asked Jadhima to send her a letter offering to come to him if she was sincere, so that he could avoid exposing himself to danger and falling in her trap. He warned Jadhima that she might avenge because he had murdered her father. However, Jadhima did not agree with him. Instead, Jadhima asked his sister's son, Amr ibn Adi, for his advice about the matter and the latter encouraged him to go ahead. Then, Jadhima deputized Amr. When Jadhima got ready, he called Qasir and asked him about his opinion. Qasir replied to him: "You left the sound opinion at Al Baqqa"; which means that he had already told him about the sound opinion there but he did not care about it.

The messengers of Al Zabba welcomed Jadhima with gifts. So, he said to Qasir: "What do you think now?". Qasir replied to him: "I feed danger". He continued his words by alerting Jadhima: "If the horsemen receiving you move in front of you, then this woman is truthful. But if they surround you, she and her people are betrayers. Thus, you will have to flee with your horse – that is called Al Asa and is so fast – and I will accompany you".

The horsemen reached Jadhima and he was not capable of riding his horse. So, Qasir rode it and fled. He run with it till the sunset to a remote land where he built a tower that was then called the Tower of Al Asa. Jadhima was murdered by Al Zabba. Qasir turned back to Amr ibn Adi and said to him: "Get ready to avenge the death of your maternal uncle soon". Amr said: "How can I overcome her while she is more powerful than an eagle".

Al Zabba asked one of her female soothsayers about her kingdom. She replied to her: "I see you will be perished because of a contemptible young man who is called Amr ibn Adi. However, you will not be perished by his hand but by your own hand, on his account". Therefore, Al Zabba began to be wary of Amr. She built a tunnel in her palace to a fortress inside her city. Then, she said: "If something abruptly occurs, I shall enter the tunnel up to my fortress". She summoned a skillful painter and said to him: "Go in disguise to Amr ibn Adi, join his retinue and mingle with them. Then, paint Amr ibn Adi in detail in all of his postures and while being fully armed as well as being disarmed. If you carried this out successfully, come back to me".

Then, the painter went ahead and carried out his task exactly according to the instructions of Al Zabba. Therefore, whenever she saw Amr ibn Adi, she recognized him whatever his guise was and took caution against him. Qasir said to Amr ibn Adi: "Let me take revenge on her". Amr replied to him: "I am not going to do so. I am more worthy of that than you". Qasir said: "Then, let me go and you will be blameless".

It was reported by ibn Al Kalbi that: The father of Al Zabba was the one who built the tunnel for her and her sister. The fortress of her sister was inside her city.

Then, Amr said to Qasir: "You are of clear sightedness". Qasir cut off his own nose and injured his own back. The Arabs said: "Qasir's cutting his nose is nothing but a ruse". Qasir went out pretending that he was fleeing. He claimed that Amr was the one who had abused him and had been plotting against his maternal uncle, Jadhima, and was gullible by Al Zabba. Then, Qasir headed to Al Zabba and caused her murder. However, there was a different narration regarding this story; that Jadhima expelled Al Zabba, then, he proposed to her. This narration is mentioned here to show the difference to the reader.

Ibn Mohammed Al Kalbi said that it was narrated by his father that: Jadhima ibn Malik was the king of Al Hirah and beyond (parts of Al Sawad). He ruled for sixty years. The Arabs and enemies were fearing him. He launched a raid to Malih ibn Baraa who was the king of Al Hadar (known as Hatra) – the barrier between the Romans and the Persians. Jadhima murdered Malih and expelled Al Zabba to the Levant. So, she went to Rome. She was an Arabic native, eloquent, of powerful rule and great zeal.

Ibn Al Kalbi said: Jesus (PBUH), the son of Mary, was sent by God after the murder of her father. She was too zealous to the extent that she mobilized troops, spent money and turned back home – the kingdom of her father. She got rid of Jadhima Al Abrash and built along the Euphrates river two cities opposite to each other from the eastern and western Euphrates. Besides, she built a tunnel between both cities under the Euphrates river to be as a refuge for her in case that an enemy burdened her. She was a virgin woman. Jadhima wished to propose to her. So, he asked his people for their opinion in this respect. Nobody answered him except his reasonable cousin, who was the warehouse and called Qasir, who justified his rejection by saying: "Al Zabba is a virgin woman who is in no need for wealth absolutely. Moreover, she wants to avenge you for killing her father but perhaps she did not take her revenge up till now for being cautious of your striking power. However, she bears deep hostility towards you. Plus, being greedy towards the ones who are of less significance than you is a matter that does not fit you. God has raised your rank".

Jadhima said: "O' Qasir, you offer good advice. However, I desire to marry her. No one can escape his destiny". Hence, he sent to her someone to tell her about his proposal. She warmly welcomed his messenger and said to him with pleasure: "I agree even though I had previously boycotted marriage out of fearing that I may not find an eligible man. In addition, the kingship is a burden greater than my eligibility and ability to bear. If a marriage proposal were not to be made by men not women, I would go to him". She also sent with him to Jadhima various gifts such as slaves and maids, arms, wealth, camels and sheep, garments … etc.

When the messenger of Jadhima turned back to him with this glad tidings, he became so pleased and thought that she agreed out of her desire in him. So, he admired himself and accordingly went to her with his trusted associates including Qasir, the ware-houser. Jadhima appointed his sister's son, Amr ibn Adi Al Lakhmi, as his successor. The latter was the first king belonging to the tribe of Lakhm over Al Hirah. His reign continued for one hundred and twenty years.

In his way to Al Zabba, he sought the advice of his associates. Qasir ibn Saad showed his objection to go to her in spite of the acceptance of the others. Qasir admonished Jadhima to be cau-tious and told him that he would advise him not to go ahead unless it was a matter of fate. Jadhima chose the view of the majority, which is compatible to his desire, and went ahead to Al Zabba. Upon his arrival, the soldiers of Al Zabba attacked him as she had previously ordered them to do. Jadhima, then, acknowledged to Qasir that his view was right. Qasir replied to him that it was too late. Then, Jadhima asked Qasir for a solution and the latter sug-gested to escape with his horse that was called Al Asa. Jadhima refused his suggestion. When Qasir found that Jadhima surren-dered to be captured and killed, he fled on the horseback of

Jadhima. Then, he turned back to Amr ibn Adi, Jadhima's sister's son, and they plotted to avenge Al Zabba.

When Amr and Qasir headed with their troops to attack Al Zabba, they killed her soldiers. Then, she moved to the tunnel she had previously built to flee through it but she found Qasir and Amr there. When she found that her death was inevitable, she preferred to commit suicide by swallowing her poisonous ring but its poison would come into effect within one hour. So, Amr and Qasir pursued and killed her with their swords. Thus, they possessed her kingdom. The biographers said: After the death of Jadhima, his sister's son, Amr ibn Adi, became the king. He was the first Arab king to dwell in Al Hirah, the first one among the Arab kings in Iraq who was glorified by the people of Al Hirah in their writings, and to whom they were related; they were the kings of the house of Nasr. Al Anbar was cultivated and populated for five hundred and fifty years till Al Hirah was cultivated and populated during the era of Amr ibn Adi.

Al Hirah was cultivated and populated for five hundred thirty years and few till the Muslims dwelled in Kufa. The reign of Amr ibn Adi continued until his death at the age of one hundred and twenty years. It was said that he died at the age of one hundred and eighty years. Some of this period fell within the era of Ardashir, and ninety and five years thereof fell within the time period of the kings of factions. Twenty three years thereof fell within the era of the kings of Persia. Fourteen years and ten months thereof fell within the era of Ardashir ibn Babak. Eighty years and two months thereof fell within the era of Shapur (also spelled Sabur) ibn Ardashir. The descendants of Amr ibn Adi continued to rule, after his death, the Arabs all over Iraq and the Hijaz desert. They were appointed by the kings of Persia until Khosrow II, who was called Parviz (which means victorious), the son of Hormizd (also spelled Hormuz), murdered Alnoaman ibn Almundhir and gave the provisions, dedicated by the kings of Persia for the Arabs, to people other than them. Alnoaman also belonged to the offspring of Nasr, because he was called Alnoaman ibn Almundhir ibn Maa Al Samaa ibn Amr ibn Adi ibn Nasr ibn Rabia.

Abu Jafar Al Tabari said: The reign of the Arab kings belonging to the house of Rabia, who were appointed by the Persian kings, continued until Amr ibn Hend came to the reign. Then, he was succeeded by his brother Qabus ibn Almundhir who ruled for four years. Eight months thereof fell within the era of Anushiruwan (also spelled Anushirvan) while three years and four months thereof fell within the era of Hormizd. Then, Sohrab came to the reign. Then, Almundhir, the father of Alnoaman ibn Almundhir, was appointed to rule for four years. Then, he was succeeded by Alnoaman ibn Almundhir, Abu Qabus, who ruled for twenty two years; seven years and eight months thereof fell within the era of

Hormizd, fourteen years and four months thereof were during the era of Parviz. Then, Iyas ibn Qabisah Al Taii ruled for nine years. Messenger of God, Mohammed (PBUH), was sent after a period of one year and eight months passed from his reign. Afterwards, he appointed Azadia Al Hamadani as his successor for seventeen years. Then, came to the reign Almundhir ibn Alnoaman ibn Almundhir for eight months until Khalid ibn Al Waleed came to Al Hirah. He was the last one of the house of Nasr. Thus, all the kings of the house of Nasr were twenty ones. They reigned for five hundred and twenty two years and eight months.

Section

Regarding the reason for the dwelling of the kings of the house of Nasr in Al Hirah

The reason for their coming to Al Hirah and dwelling there was a dream seen by Nasr ibn Rabia Al Lakhmi. His kingship was among the people of Tubba. He was terrified by the dream he had seen. So, he assembled each and every soothsayer and fortune teller. Then, he said to them: "I saw a terrifying dream. Interpret it to me". They said: "Tell us about it". He said: "Nobody can interpret it except the one who knows it prior to I narrate it". They said: "O' king, if you want so, you should bring Satih and Sheq because they are the most knowing ones". The full name of Satih was Rabi ibn Rabia ibn Masoud ibn Mazin. Sheq was called Sheq ibn Saab ibn Yashkur ibn Fahm.

So, the king sent to summon them. Satih arrived earlier than Sheq. In their era, there were no soothsayer who were more qualified than them. The king said to him: "O' Satih, I saw a terrifying dream. If you know what it is, you will interpret it well". Satih said: "You dreamed that there was a skull that got out from darkness to the land of Tihamah. Then, every creature having a skull ate from it". The king said: "O' Satih, you did not tell something wrong about it. So, how can you interpret it?". He said:" I swear by the serpent which is between the two Harras, that the Habash (Abyssinian people) will take your land from Abyn to Gurash".

The king said to him: "By your father! O' Satih, this is indeed distressing and painful, but when will this take place? During my era or afterwards?". He replied to him: "No, it will be sixty to seventy years later". The king asked: "Will their dominion last forever or will it be cut shortly?". Satih said: "No, it will be cut after little more than seventy years. Then, they will flee". The king asked: "Who will come to rule then?". Satih said: "Iram ibn Dhu Yazan who will come from Aden and expel all of them from Yemen". The king asked: "Will the dominion of Iram last forever or not?". Satih said: "It will be cut". The king asked him: "Who will reign later?". "A pure Prophet to whom God, the Most High, will send revelation". The king asked: "Who is this prophet?".

Satih said: "He is a man belonging to the descendants of Ghalib ibn Fihr ibn Malik ibn Al Nadir, whose dominion will last until the end of time". The king asked: "O' Satih, is there an end for time?". He said: "Yes, it will be the day when the earliest generations meet with the latest ones. At that time, the righteous will be blessed whereas the evildoers will be wretched". So, the king asked: "O' Satih, are you telling us the truth?". Satih said: "Yes, I swear by the redness of the dying sun at the evening, the beginning of the darkness of night and the dawn when it is breaking, what I have told you is undoubtedly true".

Sheq came later and when he was asked by king Rabia about his dream, he told the king a similar interpretation to that of Satih. When the king found that both of them gave the same interpretation, he felt that this danger will come from Habasha (Abyssinia). So, he sent his offspring and the descendants of his family to Iraq and sent a letter, on their behalf, to a Persian king called Shapur to allow them to dwell in Al Hirah. Kings still dwelled there.

Section

It was reported by the father of Al Haytham ibn Adi that:

Al Mansour, the commander of the believers, sent Al Sharqi ibn Al Qutami to serve as a tutor for Al Mahdi regarding the history of the Arabs and their good morals. Once a night, Al Mahdi asked Al Sharqi to entertain him by telling something funny. Al

Sharqi said: "I will" and told him a funny story: There was one of the kings of Al Hirah who had two close companions who joined him in all of his affairs. While he was drunk on one night, he killed them unintentionally. When he awoke, he asked about them and was informed of what he had done. So, he regretted and became full of grief for their separation. Hence, he went on a hunger strike and swore not to have a drink that can negatively affect his mind. He buried them and ordered that everybody passes by their grave should bow down before them. Al Sharqi said: "It was known that if a king introduced a certain practice, the people inherited it and the parents instructed their offspring to follow it". The people continued for a long period of time to obey the command of the king regarding bowing down before the grave of his two companions whenever they passed by it, and his command became an obligatory practice. Moreover, he judged to murder anyone who refused to bow down before that grave after being asked for giving two orders that would be executed for him whatever they were.

However, once a day, a tailor bearing his garments and clapper passed by the grave. So, he was asked by the men in charge of the grave to bow down before it but he refused to do so. Then, they warned him that he would be murdered if he did not respond. However, he insisted on his refusal. So, they took him to the king who in turn asked him about the reason of his refusal to bow down before the grave. The tailor replied to the king by saying that he already did but they were liars. The king did not believe him, told him to give two orders to be executed for him before being murdered. So, the tailor said that he ordered to strike the neck of the king with the earlier's clapper. The king sought the opinion of his ministers. They said that he should follow the practice he had introduced; that he should obey the order of the tailor, for breach of practice brought shame and subsequent breaches of other practices. Then, the king decided to give the tailor whatever he wanted even if he asked for sharing his kingdom, in order not to strike his neck. Yet, the tailor insisted on his order. After arguing too much, the king agreed. After being struck, he remained unconscious for six months. When he awoke, he asked the tailor about his second order. So, the tailor expressed that he wanted to strike the other side of the king. Upon hearing that, the king got so alarmed and was sure that he would die. He consulted his chiefs and ministers. They told him to follow the practice even he would die.

Thereupon, the king said to the tailor: "I believe that you bowed down before the grave". Then, he stood to the tailor and kissed his head; as a matter of apology. So, the tailor went out safely. Finally, Al Mahdi rejoiced greatly and said to Al Sharqi: "Well said, I swear by God". Hence, he maintained his tie and showed affection to him.

The tale of Tasm and Jadis

It was said that those tribes were during the time period of the kings of factions. The tribe of Jadis came to an end by Hassan ibn Tubba. The biographers said: The tribes of Tasm and Jadis were among the dwellers of Al Yamama. At that time, Al Yamama was one of the most fertile, cultivated and prosperous land with lofty palaces. They were ruled by a king belonging to the tribe of Tasm, who was wicked and tyrant and was called Amliq. One of his tyrannical acts they faced was his command that no virgin of the tribe of Jadis should be given to her husband until she had been brought to the king to deflower her first. Subsequently, a man belonged to the tribe of Jadis, who was called Al Aswad ibn Ghifar, said to the chief men of his people: "You can see the humiliation and shame that we suffer from. So, obey me to get rid of this shame". They asked him about what they could do. He said: "I will prepare a meal for the king and his retinue. Once they come, we will attack them with our swords. Then, I will kill him myself while everyone of you kill one of the king's retinue. Then, kill the chiefs first, thus the meanest will be nothing to worry about". They agreed with him.

They implemented the plan and murdered all of them except only one man belonging to the tribe of Tasm, because he escaped. He was called Riyah ibn Murra and fled until he reached Hassan ibn Tubba to seek his help and avenge his tribe. So, Hassan went ahead with the Himyarite troops, but when he was about to reach the region of Al Yamama by marching for three days, Riyah warned him that his sister was married in the tribe of Jadis. She was called Al Yamama and had an exceptional sight and intuition to the extent that she could see from a far distance valued by marching for three days. Riyah was afraid that she might alert her tribe with Hassan and his army. So, he advised Hassan to let every man of them hold a tree to hide behind it. So, they did. Al Yamama saw them and alerted her tribe. However, Hassan caught them in the following morning, caused their murder – including Al Yamama who was known to be the first one to apply a kohl eyeliner – and destroyed their palaces and fortresses.

Hassan was called Tubba ibn Tubba ibn Asaad Abu Karib ibn MalikiKarib. Tubba (Asaad) was claimed by the Yemeni people that he was the one who covered the Kaaba with a cloth (Kiswah) when he went to Mecca. He also provided the people there with food. He went to Yathrib (Medina) and killed the Jews there because some people of the tribes of Aws and Khazraj complained to him that the Jews were evil neighbors. It was also claimed that he sent his son Hassan to Sindh and sent Samer to Khurasan, and he ordered both of them to rush to China. Samer passed by Samarkand, so, he settled there till he conquered it. Then, he headed to China where he met Hassan. Some of the Yemini people claimed that both of them died there while some others claimed that they turned back to Tubba with wealth and spoils.

The tale of the events regarding the Persians

It was said that Alexander (Iskandar) - the Greek king - murdered Dara ibn Dara (Darius Codomanus III) who was the king of the Persians in Iraq, in the region of Babel. Then, he divided the kingdoms among the kings of factions. "The kings of factions" means that every king rules a certain region which he cannot exceed to another region. As for the land of Al Sawad, it remained under the rule of the Romans, after the death of Alexander, for fifty four years. Later on, the son of Darius the Great murdered Antiochus, the Roman king, and defeated the people of Al Sawad. And he reigned from the city of Mosul to the cities of Ray and Isfahan. Consequently, all of the other kings of factions glorified him and called him a king.

Afterwards, came to the reign the son of Ashaghan (also spelled Ashakan), and it was said ibn Shapur. It was claimed that he was the one who raided the descendants of Israel in the second time, because they murdered Prophet John, the son of Prophet Zechariah. So, God no longer made a prophet originate from among them and humiliated them. The Romans came to Persia to avenge Antiochus. At that time, the king of Babel was Balash, the father of Ardawan. He sent a letter to the kings of factions to inform them of the intention of the Romans to attack them. So, the kings mobilized troops to support him, whose number was four hundred thousand. He appointed a ruler over them from among the kings of factions beyond the end of Al Sawad to Al Hirah. He headed them until he met the king of the Romans. So, he killed him, which drove the Romans to build the city of Constantinople to which the kingship was transferred instead of Rome. Constantine the king was the one who founded Constantinople and he was the first Roman king to adopt Christianity. In addition, he was the one who expelled the remnants of the descendants of Israel from Palestine and Jordan for their killing Prophet Jesus (PBUH) - "as people falsely thought that he was killed but they killed another man who appeared like him before their eyes". He took the wooden beam which was claimed that Prophet Jesus (PBUH) was crucified on. So, the Romans glorified it and put it in their treasury. The kingship of Persia remained scattered and unsettled until Ardashir I (Ardashir ibn Babak ibn Bahman ibn Isfandiyar ibn Bishtasb) came to the reign. So, he intended to take revenge for his cousin Darius ibn Darius ibn Bahman who fought Alexander till his two gatekeepers killed him.

Ardashir sent a letter to the kings which included: From the leader of kings Ardashir ibn Babak to the one who will succeed him from among the kings of Persia. To proceed: The kings do differently from the subjects; as kingship is characterized by wealth, capacity, daring, rashness and boastfulness. Then, the longer the age of a king is and the more safe the reign is, the more the king is overwhelmed by those characteristics until he forgets about calamities, pitfalls and lessons. Consequently, he does not care about his sayings and deeds. The earlier ones said: A sensible ruler is better for the subjects than prosperity. Bear in mind that kingship and religion are twins; religion is the basis of kingship and kingship guards religion. If kingship does not adhere to religion, the earlier will be destroyed. Bear in mind that your dominion, as being kings, is over the bodies of the subjects rather than their hearts. Bear in mind that lying does not befit a king because nobody can compel him to do so. Further, he should not get angry; because anger and hostility bring evilness and remorse. Also, he should not entertain; for entertainment is a matter regarding spare time. He should not envy anyone except the kings of nations for their well governing. Bear in mind that every king has intimates, every intimate of them has other intimates and everyone of these other intimates has other intimates till all those constitute the people of the kingdom. So, if the king chooses and guides his intimates righteously, every ruler of them will do such thing with his intimates, until all of public subjects are characterized by righteousness. Bear in mind that a king may not care about his defects because the people do not talk about them, which can drive him to follow his personal inclination. So, be careful, neither reveal your secrets to the younger ones among your family nor to your servants. Bear in mind that both of the king and his subjects should not have spare time; because it will corrupt the nation and kingdom.

Section

After the death of Ardashir I, came to the reign of Persia his son Shapur I. The period of his rule was prosperous and he raided the countries. In the mountains of Tikrit between the Tigris (Dijla) river and the Euphrates (Al Furat) river there was a city called Al Hadar which was ruled by Satirun (Sanatruq II) whom the Arabs called Al Daizan. Shapur I besieged Al Hadar for four years but he did not manage to defeat Al Daizan because the latter was well fortified in his fortress. Then, the daughter of Al Daizan – who was called Al Nadirah (Nazirah) - betrayed her city to king Shapur I after seeing and falling in love with him while he was besieging the city. She revealed to him the talisman on which the ownership of the city depended, so that the city would be destroyed. Subsequently, Shapur I conquered the city by force and killed Al Daizan. Afterwards, he departed with Al Nadirah and married her. At night, he asked her, out of being astonished by her extraordinary softness, how did her father bring her up. To this, she described how well her father was treating her. Hence, Shapur I realized Al Nadirah's ingratitude towards her father and she may do the same thing with him. So, he got her killed in a brutal manner.

After Shapur I died, his son Hormizd succeeded him. The reign of Shapur I continued for thirty years (and it was said it continued for thirty one years and six months). Hormizd ruled for one year and ten days. Then, came to the reign his son Bahram ibn Hormizd (Bahram I) who was lenient, righteous and of a good life history; the course of his reign was prosperous and continued for three years and three months. Bahram ibn Bahram ibn Hormizd succeeded him and he was also of a good life history. He ruled for eighteen years, and it was said he ruled for seventeen years. Then, came to the reign Bahram ibn Bahram ibn Bahram ibn Hormizd and he was called Shahanshah (a Persian title which means king of kings). He ruled for four years. Then, came to the reign Narseh (Narsi) ibn Bahram, who was the brother of Bahram III. He was a good ruler and had a good life history for nine years. Then, came to the reign Hormizd ibn Narseh ibn Bahram ibn Bahram ibn Bahram ibn Hormizd ibn Shapur ibn Ardashir. He ruled justly and made the country prosperous for six years. Yet, it was said that he ruled for seven years. He died and left no son but his wife was pregnant. The soothsayers said that it would be a male baby and he would reign the land. So, he left a will that his awaited son should succeed him. Then, he died. So, the crown was put on the womb of his mother while he was a fetus. They named him Shapur II. He was nicknamed Shapur Dhu Al Aktaf. Nobody was known to be crowned as a king while he was in the womb of his mother except him. Then, he was born and the people rejoiced and spread the news of his delivery around. So, it became known that this nation had no king and waited for a baby in the cradle to be their king. Consequently, the Turkish people and the Romans wanted to dominate the kingship of Persia. The countries of the Arabs were the nearest countries to Persia. They were the most needy people because of poor living. So, a huge assembly of them went through the sea till they reached the district of Rostaq (also spelled Rastagh) in Persia. They seized this district including its harvest and livestock, and stayed there for a period of time. Nobody of the Persians attacked them, until Shapur II got older.

He was known of his well thought. The first evidence of that was when he found the bridge over the Tigris river be overcrowded by people, which was making noise. So, he commanded to build another bridge so that one bridge would be for the comers and the other one for those who wanted to turn back. So, the people rejoiced with his discretion in spite of his young age. His discretion still appeared until he reached the age of sixteen when he went forth at the head of one thousand warriors and killed many of the Arabs. Then, he proceeded to the land of Abd Al Qays and perished its people. Then, he proceeded to Al Yamama where he killed whoever he found, made every spring sink so deep into the ground so that nobody could seek it. He passed by the city of Yathrib and did the same ill deeds, including murder and capture. Then he turned back to Iraq. He ordered to dig a river: the beginning of which was at the city of Hit and its end was near the city of Al Qadisiyyah then to the city of Kazma then to the sea. He made over it fortresses equipped with soldiers and horses. So, whoever wanted to meet the Persian king from among the Arabs for something, should first take permission from the soldier charged with guarding the fortress that he (the Arab comer) would pass through. Then, he turned back through the same fortress he entered. Thus, the kingdom of Persia became erect and guarded against the Arabs. This river was called Al Hajiz.

Ibn Qutayba said: Shapur II was the one who built the iwan (also spelled ivan) in Al Madain and Al Sous city. He also invaded the Roman land and captured many people. He suspended hostilities with Constantine, the king of Rome. Constantine was the first one to adopt Christianity. He distributed his kingship among his three sons. Then, the Romans appointed over them a king from the household of Constantine, who was called Lulyanus. He was following the religion of the Romans that was before. However, he was concealing that and pretending to be a Christian, before he came to the reign. Yet, after he became a king, he declared the religion of the Romans and ordered them to revive it. He also ordered to destroy churches and kill the Bishops and the

Christian rabbis. Moreover, he mobilized an army from among the Romans and the Khazars in addition to the Arabs who were settling in his kingdom in order to fight Shapur II and the troops of Persia.

Therefore, the Arabs seized the opportunity to take revenge on Shapur II for the Arabs he had killed. The Arab army of Lulyanus was composed of one hundred and seventy thousand troopers. He dispatched them headed by a man from among the Roman patricii, who was called Yusanus. Lulyanus went forth until he reached Persia. When Shapur II learnt this news, he became terrified and sent spies to them. However, the spies brought different news to Shapur II. So, he went forth in disguise along with his trusted people to inspect the army of his enemy by himself. When he approached the army of Yusanus who was appointed by Lulyanus as the head of his army, Shapur II sent a troop to it to bring him the real news. So, the Romans captured them and took them to Yusanus, but none of the troop confessed of the reason behind their coming except one man. He told Yusanus about the whole matter as well as the place of Shapur II. This man asked Yusanus to send some of his troopers with him to deliver them Shapur II. So, Yusanus sent a man from among his intimates to Shapur II to warn him. Consequently, Shapur II departed from his spot and turned back to his army. Then, the Arabs went ahead and fought Shapur II. They killed too much of his troopers and Shapur II fled with the remnants of his army. Lulyanus seized the city of Shapur II and took over his treasuries. Shapur II sent a letter to his troopers who were far away to inform them of what he had faced and to order them to support him. So, the armies were mobilized to support him. Thus, he went forth to fight Lulyanus and recovered his land from him.

Once a day, Lulyanus was killed by an arrow shot at him by an unknown person. So, his troopers got confused and asked Yusanus to be a king over them. However, he refused and said: "I adopt the religion of Christianity whereas the chiefs are against this religion". So, the Romans told him that they adopted his religion but they were concealing this for fearing Lulyanus. Hence, they appointed him as their king and declared Christianity. When Shapur II knew about the death of Lulyanus, he sent to the leaders of the Roman troopers asking them for bringing him one chief amongst them. So, Yusanus came to him at the head of eighty men. Accordingly, Shapur II welcomed and hugged him as a gratitude for his response to his call. Shapur II sent a letter to the leaders of the Roman troopers telling them: "If you were to appoint a king other than Yusanus, you would be perished. Rather, his kingship over you is the cause of your rescue".

Yusanus became more dominant. Then, he said: "the Romans killed a lot of people in our land and destroyed its prosperity. So, either shall they pay to us for their corruption or shall they compensate us for that by giving us the city of Nusaybin belonging to the land of Persia that the Romans had dominated. So, they gave up to him the city of Nusaybin. When this news reached its people, they left it for knowing that Shapur II was against their religion. Then, Shapur II moved twelve thousand houses from the people of Istakhr and Isfahan and other cities into Nusaybin. Yusanus went away to the Roman kingdom. He settled there for a short while before his death. Shapur II fought the Arabs severely and perished their rulers, ripping out their shoulders. Therefore, he was nicknamed Dhu Al Aktaf (The man of the shoulders).

Some scholars mentioned: When Shapur II damaged the Arabs and expelled them from the regions of Persia, Bahrain and Yamama, he went to the Levant and Rome. He informed his associates that he intended to enter Rome to inspect the Roman secrets. So, he entered there and he was told that Caesar (the king of Rome) gave a banquet and assembled the people for it. So, Shapur II went to that assembly to see Caesar. However, Shapur II was recognized and captured. Caesar went forth along with his troopers to the land of Persia, accompanying Shapur II who was captured and put into a bull skin. Caesar killed too much people and destroyed the cities until he reached the city of Gondishapur whose people were well fortified. So, he set up catapults and destroyed parts of the city. Meanwhile, once a day, the Roman soldiers who were in charge of supervising Shapur II were inattentive to him, and some captives of the city of Ahvaz were near him, he ordered them to throw oil at the bull skin he was captured within. So, they did and the skin became soften and he was freed accordingly. He still moved forward until he approached the gate of the city and informed its gatekeepers of his name. So, he entered the city and its people warmly welcomed him and praised God in a loud voice. Hence, the associates of Caesar heard their sounds. Shapur II mobilized the people who were in the city and went forth to the Romans at night. He killed them and left Rome, capturing Caesar, chaining him and taking over his wealth and women as spoils. He then reconstructed what Caesar had destroyed. Then, he killed his offspring and sent him to Rome over a donkey. Afterwards, Shapur II settled for a period of time. Then, he raided Rome, killed some people and captured others. Then, he deemed the Arabs good and made some of them dwell in the cities of Ahvaz and Kerman. His reign continued for seventy two years.

Section

During the era of Shapur II, Mani who was a Zendik (which means an apostate) appeared. Yahia ibn Bishr ibn Omayr Al Nahawandi said: "Mani was one of the senior Christian Bishops. He was known of a good life history among them. Nevertheless, he committed unlawful sexual intercourse during the era of Shapur

II, Dhu Al Aktaf, the king of Persia. Thus, his rank in Christianity fell down. His archbishop peers had been bearing envy towards him but when he committed that sin, they seized the opportunity to fulfill their wish of overthrowing him. Accordingly, he began to defend himself against his associates saying: "I did not commit unlawful sexual intercourse but the people of the monastery envied me and rejected that I am against their religion; since they used to believe in the Theological Jesus and follow the ordained ways of Prophet Jesus, the son of Mary". Then, he wrote a book in which he calumniated the most determined ones of the Messengers. Moreover, he tended to follow the law of the Magians who believed that Abraham, Moses and Jesus were the messengers of the deity of darkness, not the messengers of God. So, Mani supported their claim.

He set out faulty laws for his associates. In addition, he wrote a book dedicated for Shapur II and entitled it "Shapuragan" in which he explained his doctrine. As a result, Shapur II followed him. However, the advocators of Shapur II rejected that. So, they said to Shapur II: "Mani says that you are a devil. If you wish, you can ask him who has created your hand?". Shapur II asked Mani this question on which the latter replied that the devil was the one who created it. So, Shapur II rejected that and ordered his men to crucify Mani. So, they did till he died. Afterwards, one of his learners, called Kushta, succeeded him. So, the doctrine of Mani got strengthened.

During the era of Shapur II, the ruler he had appointed over the tribes of Mudhar and Rabia died. He was called Imru Al Qays ibn Amr ibn Adi ibn Rabia ibn Nasr. So, Shapur II appointed his son Amr ibn Imru Al Qays instead.

Upon the death of Shapur II, he willed that his brother, Ardashir ibn Hormizd ibn Narseh ibn Bahram ibn Hormizd ibn Shapur ibn Ardashir ibn Babak, would succeed him. When his reign got stabilized for him, he killed a lot of scholars and rulers. So, the people ousted him four years after his coming to reign. Then, Shapur ibn Shapur II Dhu Al Aktaf ruled. So, it was a glad tidings to the subjects that he recovered the kingship of his father. He was lenient and ordered the others to be so. His ousted uncle, Ardashir, succumbed to him. During his era, Amr ibn Imru Al Qays died. So, Shapur appointed Aws ibn Qallam, who was one of the Amalekites, instead. The great men of the state and the members of noble houses cut the ropes of a large tent erected for Shapur. So, the tent fell down on him and killed him immediately. The reign of Shapur continued for five years.

Then, came to the reign his brother, Bahram ibn Shapur II Dhu Al Aktaf. He was called Kerman Shah since his father had made him the ruler of Kerman during his lifetime. He sent a letter to the leaders of his army urging them to obedience. He built a city at

Kerman. His rule was commendable. During his era, Aws ibn Qallam, who was ruling the Arabs, died. He ruled for five years – and it is said that his name was Yaws, which is more accurately – so Imru Al Qays ibn Amr ibn Imru Al Qays ibn Amr ibn Adi was his successor. The reign of Bahram continued for eleven years. Then, one of the murderers rose against him and killed him by shooting an arrow at him.

Then, came to the reign after him Yazdajird, who was called "the Sinful One". Some scholars said that he was the son of the king killed before him. On the other hand, others said that he was his brother. He was rough, harsh and of a negative character. He imposed a severe penalty on the weak, that no one could bear, and shed blood. That's why he was called "the Sinful One", since the kings of Persia used to be fair but he was not. So, the people sought the protection of God, Exalted is He, from this tyrant king and supplicated God to hasten retribution for him. Once a day, while he was in the city of Gorgan, a fast, unparalleled horse came and stopped at his gate, which astonished the people. When Yazdajird was told about it, he ordered to saddle and bridle it. His groomers tried to do so but they failed. So, he went out, saddled and bridled it himself. The horse did not move. Then, it suddenly struck him on his heart so that he died. Subsequently, the horse fled and nobody could catch it. The subjects said: "God, Exalted is He, is Most Compassionate to us". The reign of this tyrant continued for twenty two years, five months and sixteen days. It was said that he reigned for twenty one years, five months and eighteen days.

During the era of Yazdajird, Imru Al Qays ibn Amr ibn Imru Al Qays died. His successor was his son, Alnoaman ibn Imru Al Qays ibn Amr ibn Adi, and he was the one who built the palace of Al Khawarnaq. The reason for building Al Khawarnaq palace was that Yazdajird, the Sinful One, had no surviving son. Hence, when his son Bahram was born to him, he asked about a healthy dwelling free from diseases. He was guided to the upper part of Al Hirah. So, he sent his son Bahram Gur (Jur) to Alnoaman and ordered the latter to build the palace of Al Khawarnaq to be a residence for Bahram. The one who actually built the palace of Al Khawarnaq was called Sinnimar who was brought from Rome because he was famous for building fortresses and palaces for kings. Sinnimar built Al Khawarnaq palace within two years. When he accomplished the construction, Alnoaman and his minister were amazed at it because they could see the earth and the sea from the top of it. So, Sinnimar cunningly said to Alnoaman in order to come close to him: "I know the place of a brick if it is removed, the whole building will be destroyed". So, Alnoaman replied to him: "There is no need to know its place as long as nobody knows it". Then, he ordered to throw Sinnimar from the top of the building so he died.

There was another narration regarding that event: When Al-noaman and his minister were amazed at the beauty of the building and the perfection of its construction, Sinnimar said to Alnoaman: "If I knew that you would pay me my due wage and grant me what I deserve, I would have constructed a building which would have gone round with the sun wherever it went". Alnoaman replied to him: "This means that you could have constructed a building superior to this, yet you did not do it!". As a result, he ordered to throw Sinnimar from the top of Al Khawarnaq palace and he died accordingly. Thus, the Arabs created a proverb concerning that by saying: "That was the reward of Sinnimar".

Alnoaman frequently raided the Levant and captured people and spoils. He was the best king to subdue his enemy. The king of Persia provided him with two battalions: One was called Dawsar which belonged to the tribe of Tanukh while the other was Al shahbaa which belonged to Persia. Thus, he used to raid the Levant and the ones who did not subject to him from among the Arabs, being supported with these two battalions.

Once a day during Spring, Alnoaman was sitting in his chamber at Al Khawarnaq palace where he was able to see Al Najaf city along with what were beyond it: the orchards, date palms and rivers on the western side, and see the Euphrates river on the eastern side. So, he was pleased with the greenery and rivers. Then, he said to his minister: "Have you ever seen such a view?!". His minister replied to him: "No. If it were to last forever!". Alnoaman asked: "What then lasts forever?". His minister replied to him: "It is that which is with God in the Afterlife". Alnoaman asked: "How can that be attained?". His minister replied to him: "By abandoning the pleasures of this worldly life and worshipping God". Hence, Alnoaman forsook his kingdom at the same night. He wore coarse garments and left secretly. Next morning, the people could know nothing about him. The reign of Alnoaman continued until he forsook it and he wandered around the globe for twenty nine years and four months. Among that period were fifteen years during the era of Yazdajird, and fourteen years were during the era of Bahram Gur ibn Yazdajird.

It was said: Bahram Gur succeeded his father, Yazdajird, as a king. His full name was Bahram Gur ibn Yazdajird ibn Bahram Kerman Shah ibn Shapur II Dhu Al Aktaf. When Bahram was born, his father ordered the soothsayers to tell him about the future of his son. So, they told him that he should be brought among the Arabs. So, Yazdajird summoned Almundhir ibn Alnoaman, honored him and made him a king over the Arabs. He also ordered him to accompany Bahram to the land of the Arabs. So, Almundhir took Bahram to his own residence. He selected three women, characterized by strong body, bright mind and good morals and belonged to the nobles, to breast feed him alternatively.

When Bahram reached the age of five years, he told Almundhir: "Bring me tutors endued with knowledge and experience to teach me writing, shooting and jurisprudence". Yet, Almundhir said to him: "You are still young". Bahram replied to him: "I am young in age but of an intelligent mind like an adult. Knowledge is the most primary demand for kings. So, hasten the response to my request".

So, Almundhir rushed to bring him a group of Persian jurists, shooting and writing tutors. He also summoned Arab wise men and lecturers to keep close to Bahram. He allocated a certain appointment for every one of them to teach Bahram. The latter benefited a lot from them, till he reached the age of twelve years, to the extent that he excelled his tutors and they acknowledged his favor upon them. Bahram rewarded Almundhir as well as his tutors and ordered them to leave him alone, except the tutors of shooting and chivalry. Then, Bahram turned back to his father but the latter used to not to care about a son. So, he made Bahram a servant for him and this strained Bahram.

Afterwards, a brother of Caesar, who was called Thiadhos, came to Yazdajird asking for suspension of hostilities and reconciliation. Then, Bahram asked his father for a permission to go to Almundhir. So, he allowed him to go. Bahram went forth to the land of the Arabs and tended to pleasures. Yazdajird died during the absence of Bahram. The great men of the state and the members of noble houses covenanted with each other not to appoint as a king anyone from among the offspring of Yazdajird because of his bad life history. They said that Bahram was the only son of Yazdajird who might come to the reign. And they did not know him well as he never ruled before. In addition, his manners were like that of the Arabs, because he was brought amongst them, not of the Ajam. Therefore, they agreed with the public to give the kingship to a man, called Khorsow, belonging to the offspring of Ardashir ibn Babak. They immediately appointed him on the same day they decided so. When Bahram learnt the news of the death of his father and the appointment of Khorsow as a king, he summoned Almundhir and his son Alnoaman in addition to some people of the noblest Arabs. He told them: "I do not suppose that you deny the favors of my father; he did good to you, assembly of the Arabs, and was tough against the Persians". Then, he informed them of the news that reached him.

Almundhir said to Bahram: "Do not worry. I will develop a plan". Subsequently, Almundhir mobilized ten thousand Arab troopers and dispatched them headed with his son to two cities belonging to the king. He ordered him to camp near these two cities and to regularly send his heralds there. He fought anybody that was about to fight him. He raided anybody advocating those cities and captured some people but forbade his troopers to shed blood. Alnoaman went forth till he dwelled near the two cities and sent his heralds there. Accordingly, he found that fighting the Persians would be hard. A messenger was sent by the great men of the state and the members of noble houses to Almundhir to inform him of the situation of Alnoaman. So, Almundhir ordered the messenger to meet king Bahram. When the messenger turned back to Almundhir after meeting Bahram, he advised Almundhir to go accompanied with Bahram to discuss the matter with the great men and the members of noble houses.

Thus, Almundhir got ready and went forth with Bahram at the head of thirty thousand Arab troopers, who were given strength to vehement war, to the two cities of the king. When they arrived, Almundhir ordered to gather the people before him and Bahram. The great Persians and the members of noble houses began to talk to Almundhir, telling him in detail about the bad manners of Yazdajird, the father of Bahram, and that he destroyed the land by his dim view. Besides, he committed a lot of murders unjustly to the extent that he killed the people in the countries he ruled. Moreover, he did so many awful deeds other than that. They also said that they covenanted with each other not to appoint the son of Yazdajird as their king for those reasons. Then, they asked Almundhir not to compel them to a king that they abhorred.

So, Almundhir apprehended what they said and told Bahram: "You are more entitled to respond to them than me". Bahram said to them: "I was also detesting his deeds (meaning his father) and

I hope to fix what he had corrupted. If a year passes after I rule without fulfilling my covenant to you, I will forsake kingship willingly. I call God to witness about that. However, I accept that you put the crown between two savage lions and the one who manages to take the crown from among them, will be appointed by you as a king". They accepted his suggestion and told him: "You and Khorsow should seek to seize the crown from among the two lions. The one who succeeds to seize it, will be appointed by us as the king". So, Bahram agreed. Then, Bahram said to Khorsow: "The crown is near you". Khorsow replied to him: "You are more deserving to be the king than me; because you seek kingship out of inheritance whereas I am forced to it". Bahram did not get annoyed of what Khorsow said and moved towards the crown, fighting the two lions courageously. He was enabled to take over the crown. So, all the people willingly submitted to him and accepted him to be their king. At that time, he was only twenty years old.

He continued to promise the people of prosperity and commanded them to be pious and obedient to God, the Almighty and Sublime, for seven subsequent days. Then, he preferred amusement. So, his subjects blamed him a lot. The kings of the countries around became greedy to take over his land. The first one who plotted against him was Khagan, the king of the Turkish. He raided him at the head of fifty thousand and two hundred Turkish troopers. When that news reached the Persians, they got terrified. So, a group of leaders came to Bahram and told him: "You must be engaged with the disturbing news rather than amusement"; but he did not care about them and did not forsake amusement.

Then, he got equipped and went out to the country of Azerbaijan for worship and to move then to Armenia to amuse there with hunting. He was accompanied by seven leaders from among the great ones of the state, the members of noble houses and three hundred men given strength to vehement war. He appointed his brother, who was called Narseh, as his successor over his kingship. Upon knowing the travel of Bahram, the people did not suspect that he did so for fleeing his enemy. Hence, they conspired to send a delegation to Khagan in order to inform him that they would pay a land tax. They did so for fearing that he would seize their land and fight them. So, when Khagan learnt that, he secured their land. The spy that was sent by Bahram to Khagan turned back to Bahram and told him about the determination of Khagan. So, Bahram headed to him along with his army and killed Khagan by himself. He also killed a lot of his troopers. The remnant troopers were defeated and retreated to their land but Bahram pursued them to kill them and seize captives and spoils. Bahram attained the crown of Khagan and overwhelmed his country belonging to the Turkish land. Consequently, some people from the nearby countries came to Bahram in submission.

They asked him to inform them of the boundary between him and them in order not to transgress it. So, he assigned a boundary and built a lighthouse for them. He dispatched one of his leaders to the river beyond them. This leader fought the people there till they confessed to Bahram that they would be his slaves and would pay him a poll tax.

Bahram turned back to Azerbaijan. Then, he went forth to the city of Ctesiphon and he settled his kingdom there. Afterwards, he sent a letter to his troopers and his rulers entitled by him to inform them that he had killed Khagan. Then, he appointed his brother, Narseh, as the ruler of Khorasan and ordered him to dwell in the city of Balkh.

It was mentioned that after Bahram had raided the Turkish, he delivered a speech to the people of his kingdom for subsequent days; in which he urged them to constant obedience and informed them that he intended to make their land prosperous. He also warned them that if they diverted from righteousness, they would experience more harshness than that of his father. He also told them that his father was lenient and fair towards them at the be-ginning of his rule. Then, they denied that. So, he became tough towards them accordingly. Afterwards, he abolished land tax for three years to thank God for overcoming enemies. In addition, he gave the poor and needy a lot of funds. He also gave the members of noble houses and persons of meritorious behavior twenty million dirhams.

Bahram entered the land of India in disguise and stayed there for a period of time. Thereupon, he was told that an elephant somewhere in India killed a lot of people. So, he asked about its place and went forth to kill it. When that news reached the king of India, he rewarded Bahram with a great wealth. Then, the king asked Bahram about himself. So, Bahram said: "I am one of the great Persians. The king of Persia got angry with me, so, I fled to you". Then, one enemy invaded the king of India and the latter was about to succumb to him. Yet, Bahram forbade the Indian king to do that. Furthermore, he went forth to fight the enemy and defeated him. So, the king married him to his daughter. Moreover, he granted him Debal, Makran and the lands beyond it from Sindh. The king ordered to combine those countries to the land of the Ajam. So, Bahram left well pleased. Then, he went forth to the land of Sudan from the side of Yemen. He conquered it, killed and captured a huge number of its people. Then, he turned back to his kingdom.

Bahram had a son whom he planned to succeed him. However, he found his son as being deficient. Therefore, he commissioned tutors and wise men to instruct him. Nevertheless, they got desperate of making him be of good manners. There was an old man who was decent, wise and well-knowledged in Khorasan. He advised people to love; because love motivates Man to care about himself, dress well, be active, witty and enthusiastic. Yet, he instructed them to beware the forbidden matters. He meant to love by a lawful way; such as marriage. When he was asked about the reason for his advice of love, he told the story of Bahram Gur and his son. The latter became of good manners when he loved a girl who refused to marry him unless he became eligible for kingship. His father was the one who asked her – through her father - to do that in order to discipline his son. So, when the son knew the reason for her refusal to his proposal, he began to be decent, seek wisdom, knowledge, chivalry and shooting and cared about his appearance beside accompanying good associates. Consequently, the king became pleased and married him to the girl. In addition, he instructed his son regarding his wife saying: "Treat her in the best manner because she made you a favor of reaching this high moral standing of kings to the extent that you become eligible to be my successor. Hence, honor her as much as you can". The son obeyed his father and both were pleased. Bahram rewarded and honored the girl's father. Further, he willed that his son would be his successor.

There were different sayings concerning the period of the reign of Bahram. Some people said that his reign continued for eighteen years, ten months and twenty days. Others said that his reign continued for twenty three years, ten months and twenty days.

Then, came to the reign his son, Yazdajird ibn Bahram Gur. When he was crowned, the nobles met him to congratulate and supplicate God for him. He replied well to them and he referred to his father and his fine life history. He used to be kind to his subjects and do good to them while being suppressive towards his enemy. He had two sons: one was called Hormizd who was the king of Sistan, and the other son was called Fayruz. Hormizd overwhelmed the kingship after the death of his father Yazdajird. So, Fayruz fled him to the empire of the Hephthalites. He informed its king of what had happened and that he was more deserving to rule than his brother Hormizd. He asked the king to support him with an army to fight Hormizd. The king rejected until he was informed that Hormizd was a tyrant. So, he said: "Tyranny does not please God". Thus, he supported Fayruz with an army. Fayruz fought his brother Hormizd, killed him and overwhelmed the kingship. The reign of Yazdajird continued for eighteen years and four months. However, it was said that it continued for seventeen years.

Then, Fayruz ibn Yazdajird ibn Bahram Gur reigned after he had killed his brother. Yet, it was said that he imprisoned him when he overcame him. He judged justly and divided funds among the people during a time of dearth. Afterwards, he fought the Hephthalites who had previously supported him to fight his brother. He was killed during the battle accordingly. On the other hand, it was said that he fell down into a trench so that he died. His reign continued for twenty six years. Others said that it continued for twenty one years.

Then, his son, Balash ibn Fayruz, succeeded him to the reign. Kavad I had fought him for the kingship. It ended with the victory of Balash and the fleeing of Kavad I to the king of the Turkish. Balash was constantly of a praiseworthy life history. He cared so much about his subjects to the extent that if he learnt that a house was destroyed and its dwellers went away from it, he would punish the local governor of the village where that house was located, for he (the governor) had overlooked them until they became compelled to go away. He built a city, called today Sabat, in Al Sawad. It was near Al Madain. His reign continued for four years.

Then, came to the reign his brother, Kavad I ibn Fayruz. When Kavad I escaped from his brother, Balash, to the king of the Turkish with a little group, he desired to marry. So, Zarmehr recommended a very beautiful girl whose father was a noble knight. He married her and she became pregnant with Anushiruwan. So, he rewarded and loved her ardently. Afterwards, the king of the Turkish dispatched an army with him. So, he went out and asked about his wife. So, he was told that she gave birth to a male baby. When he saw the baby, he found him look exactly like him. Then, he was informed of the death of Balash. So, he saw a good omen in the born baby. When he, along with his family, went to

Al Madain and his kingship became of dominant power, he built the city of Arrajan, the city of Holwan and a lot of cities. After ten years passed of the period of his reign, they wanted to oust him from the kingship; because he followed a man called Mazdak ibn Marda.

Mazdak was calling the people to the religion of Zoroaster. He claimed that he was the prophet of the Magians. Mazdak used to wear garments made of wool, to be an ascetic and pray more for the sake of being close to the public. He along with his companions were claiming that the one who had an overabundance of wealth, luggage and women should give it to others. He claimed that doing so was a righteousness which God would be pleased with and reward for it. Thus, the lowly people seized that opportunity and followed Mazdak with his companions. They broke through the house of anyone and took by force his wealth and wife. They made Kavad I follow their way. Kavad I was the best one among their kings until Mazdak affected him. The people were afflicted with Mazdak and his followers whose negative impact became dominant.

Then, Zarmehr went forth with his noble followers to kill the followers of Mazdak. So, he killed a lot of them. Then, the remnants of them stir Kavad I up against Zarmehr. So, Kavad I killed him. Then, he raided Rome and built the city of Amida. Then,

Kavad I left a will to his son Khorsow to be his successor. He died after he had reigned for forty three years.

Then, came to the reign Khorsow Anushiruwan ibn Kavad I ibn Fayruz ibn Yazdajird ibn Bahram Gur. He ruled seriously with a firm will. He learnt about the life history of Ardashir and followed suit. He also checked the policies of the previous nations and selected what pleased him. He appointed a group of rulers over the countries and supported the fighters with weapons and horses. He was enabled to recover some countries which were seized in the Persian kingdom. He was told that a faction from the Arabs raided the boundaries of Al Sawad that he reigned. So, he ordered to dig the river that was called Al Hajiz (which means the barrier). He was known among people of his sound opinion, seriousness, good knowledge and might as well as leniency.

When he was crowned as a king, the noble men met him and supplicated God for him. So, he began his speech with remembering the blessing of God upon His mankind when He created them; His ruling their affairs and measuring out varied provisions for all of them. Then, he informed the people of their affliction with the loss of their religion and the corruption of their affairs concerning their offspring and the means of livelihood. He promised them that he would reform their affairs. Afterwards, he ordered to kill the followers of Mazdak and abolish the religion of Zoroaster that was the heresy he originated among Magianism during the era of Vishtaspa.

Anushiruwan killed and crucified one hundred thousand of the Zindiq all at once from Jazar to Al Nahrawan and Al Madain. He gave their wealth to the needy. He also killed the ones who had taken by force the property of people and rendered it back to their rightful owners. He compelled every man who had raped a woman to give her dowry. Then, he let the woman choose either marrying this man or marrying another one, except if she was already a wife, so she would return to her husband. Besides, he ordered to punish everyone who had seized something unlawfully and forced them to render it back. He allocated some money of the Public treasury – Bait Al Mal – for the trousseau of the orphan women and married them to members of noble houses. In addition, he ordered to dig rivers and canals, rebuild every broken bridge or arch or ruined village. He also built palaces and fortresses. Moreover, he appointed the best rulers and leaders. He sent one of the wise men to India to bring him a copy of the book entitled "Kalila and Demna" seeking the wisdom therein. When his kingship became of dominant power and the countries succumbed to him, he moved towards Antakya after two years passed of his reign. In Antakya, there were the great troopers of Caesar. However, he conquered it. Then, he ordered to get the city of Antakya portrayed in detail to build a city similar to it beside Al

Madain. So, the city of Rome was built in the same way as Antakya. Then, he made the people of Antakya dwell in Rome.

Consequently, when they entered to the city of Rome, they found its houses similar to their own ones in Antakya. So, everybody went to the house similar to his own previous house as if they did not leave Antakya. Afterwards, he directed to the city of Heraclius and conquered it. Then, he conquered Alexandria and beyond. He left behind some soldiers of his army in Rome after Caesar had submitted to him. Then, he went forth to the Khazars and recovered his subjects that had been oppressed by them. Subsequently, he went forth to Aden and killed the great men there. Then, he moved to Al Madain and honored Almundhir ibn Al-noaman, appointing him as a king over the Arabs. Then, he went to the Hephthalites, to take revenge for his grandfather Fayruz whom they had killed in the past. Furthermore, he rebuilt the iwan.

The reason for rebuilding the iwan

Once a day, while Khosrow Anushiruwan was sitting in his old iwan, he suddenly saw a flower. He went to the orchard to bring it. When he was about to pick it, the iwan got destroyed. So, he knew that God, the Almighty and Sublime, is Most Subtle towards His creatures. Hence, he was so astonished and pleased and he largely gave in charity. Then, he reconstructed the iwan in a more better way than its old building.

When he accomplished its construction, he raised his head up one day and saw a pigeon. He also saw a huge snake that was about to attack the pigeon and eat it. Therefore, he threw the arch at the snake and it was killed as a result. The pigeon flied safely. He rejoiced for doing good to it. Five days later, the pigeon came and sat on the window. It began to throw unknown seeds while Anushiruwan was watching it. So, he planted these seeds in his orchard and a good smell plant grew. He then said: "It is the reward of the pigeon for we have saved its life. A good deed really does not go in vain. I ask God, who has inspired this bird with the means to thank us, to inspire our subjects to be grateful to us for defending and saving them from ruining their religion and worldly life, and to inspire us to be patient with doing good to them constantly".

His life was full of ongoing victories and he was respected by all nations. In addition, a great number of delegations of the Turkish, Chinese and Khazars came to him. Anushiruwan used to honor the scholars. His reign continued for forty eight years. Also, it was said that he ruled for forty seven years, eight months and ten days.

Tale of some of his news

It was written on the bed of Khosrow Anushiruwan: "The religion will not be fully ruled with except if supported by kingship. Kingship will not be completed except by men. Men will not be powerful without wealth. Wealth will not be obtained except by constructing the earth. Construction will not be accomplished except by justice". It was also written on the side of his bed: "Ruling justly is more beneficial for the subjects than fertility". Khosrow received a complaint that the land tax collector in the city of Ahvaz collected more than the amount required by eight thousand dirhams. So, Khosrow ordered to repay the fund and he said: "If the king fills his Public treasuries with the funds taken from his subjects, he thus looks like the one who constructs the roof of his house by what will destroy its foundations". Khosrow lost his son but he did not feel dismayed. When he was asked about the reason for that, he said: "It is a matter of absolute ignorance to make heart engaged with something that will never come back".

One of his famous quotes was: "Distress strikes mind and temper and leads to helplessness. If a reasonable man faces something that requires a plan, grief will be gone and mind will be able to plan". A further quote attributed to him was: "To possess a little while being less distressed is more blessing than possessing a lot while being unkind". He also said that he preferred obeying God to possessing a lot. In addition, he mentioned that he studied the biographies of Rome and India and picked the commended matters thereof. He assured that the most harmful thing for kings was a disdain to knowledge.

It was reported by Al Asmaii that Khosrow Anushiruwan had two golden vessels in which he ate. One of his associates stole one vessel while Khosrow was watching him. When the chef searched for it, Khosrow said to him: "Do not care about it. The one who stole it will not render it back and the one who saw him stealing will not disclose his fault". When that robber came to Khosrow later on, having his sword and girdle adorned with gold, Khosrow said to him in Persian: "Sell me the sword and girdle". The man agreed and nobody grasped that matter except both of them.

Ibrahim ibn Abd Al Samad narrated: When Khosrow Anushiruwan dug the canal called Al Qatul, it harmed the meanest; they suffered drought until they became so poor. Therefore, the people of this village came out to Khosrow to complain their suffering. They met him on the way and complained to him of himself. So, he insisted on sitting on the ground as long as they said that he was unfair to them. Upon listening to their complaint, he told them that he would order to block the canal. However, they rejected his decision for this would not fit him. They suggested instead to build for them a stream over Al Qatul. He agreed and their village prospered accordingly.

Khosrow Anushiruwan said: "I fear that someone wronged by me cannot get to me". So, he hanged bells over a curtain near his house and ordered a herald to announce to the people that if anyone had been wronged, they should move this curtain.

Among the events took place during his era:

Khosrow Anushiruwan was informed that there was a man in the city of Nishapur who looked like him and was called Anushiruwan as well. He was a weaver and born on the same day and time as that of Khosrow Anushiruwan. So, the latter sent two trusted, religious men to the city of Nishapur to bring him details about that man. The two men sent a letter to Khosrow telling him that the weaver was truthful, righteous and adhering to the straight path to the extent that nobody of his profession matched him. Consequently, Khosrow Anushiruwan got astonished and ordered to pay this weaver ten thousand dirhams every year. Moreover, he let him decide not to work as a weaver if he wished and he would be paid more than he needed. The ruler of Nishapur gave the money to the weaver and informed him of the decisions of Khosrow Anushiruwan concerning him. He replied that he could not breach the practice of Khosrow by giving up work relying on his fund. He added that were it not for the bless I got for being named after Khosrow, I would change my name, for that a man like me should not be named after the king. When his reply reached Khosrow Anushiruwan, the latter ordered to appoint

Anushiruwan, the weaver, as the chief of weavers. So, he got a lot of wealth and did not give up his work. He died in the same year when Khosrow Anushiruwan died.

Among the events took place during the era of Khosrow Anushiruwan:

Khosrow Anushiruwan ordered his troopers not to encroach upon the vegetation of anyone. However, one of those troopers passed by a watermelon field and took one. The owner of the field saw him and insisted on taking him to Khosrow. So, the trooper proposed to him one thousand dirhams but he rejected. Then, the earlier added the sum to ten thousand dirhams but he rejected again. When they went to Khosrow and told him the story, he blamed the trooper who in turn assured that he did not possess other than that sum. Then, Khosrow asked the cultivator astonishingly about the reason behind his rejecting ten thousand dirhams and his desire to kill this distressed trooper. The cultivator replied that he did not desire to kill the trooper and that he was poor and did not experience prosperity except in the epoch of Khosrow. He clarified that he did so to add to the dignity of Khosrow's deeds so that the news would spread that a watermelon cost ten thousand dirhams in his epoch. Hence, Khosrow approved his words and ordered the trooper to give him the money.

Among the events took place during the era of Khosrow Anushiruwan:

There was the birth of Abdullah ibn Abd Al Muttalib – the father of our Prophet Mohammed (PBUH). Abdullah was born in the fifteen year during the reign of Anushiruwan. Our Prophet Mohammed (PBUH) was born in the forty year of his reign, and it was the Year of the Elephant.

Among the events took place during the era of Khosrow Anushiruwan:

The kingship of Yemen continued for a long period of time. Nobody was greedy to take over it until Abyssinia raided Yemen during the era of Anushiruwan.

Hisham ibn Mohammed said: The Abyssinians did so because Dhu Nuwas Al Himyari, the king of Yemen during that epoch, was a Jewish. So, one Jewish man of the people of Najran, called Daws, came and told him that the people of Najran had killed his two daughters unjustly. Therefore, he sought the help of the Yemeni king. The people of Najran were Christians. So, Dhu Nuwas advocated Judaism. He raided the people of Najran and killed a lot of them. Then, a man among the people of Najran went to the king of Abyssinia to inform him of their disaster. In addition, he gave him the Gospel some of which was fired. The king said to him: "I have many troopers but do not have ships. So, I will send a letter to Caesar of Rome to send me ships to carry the troopers". So, he sent to Caesar a letter and the fired Gospel. As a result, Caesar sent to him a lot of ships. The king of Abyssinia sent an army of seventy thousand Abyssinians headed by an Abyssinian called Aryat to Yemen. The king instructed this leader to kill one third of the Yemeni, destroy one third of their country and capture one third of their women and offspring. So, Aryat went forth at the head of his troopers among which was Abraha Al Ashram through the sea to Yemen. Subsequently, Dhu Nuwas heard about that news. So, he mobilized the men of Himyar along with the tribes of Yemen which obeyed him. Then, Dhu Nuwas got defeated and Aryat conquered Yemen with his troopers. Thereupon, Dhu Nuwas proceeded on his horse towards the sea then he struck it, so, it moved fast with him in a sand dune till he died. It was claimed that he drowned in the sea.

When Aryat entered Yemen at the head of the Abyssinian army, he obeyed the above mentioned commands of Alnagashi – meaning the king of Abyssinia – and sent to him one third of the captives. Then, he appointed Abraha as the king of Sanaa – the capital of Yemen – and other Yemeni governorates. However, Aryat did not inform Alnagashi of that. So, Alnagashi was told that: "Aryat defected from your obedience and he considered himself in no need of you". Consequently, Alnagashi directed an army to raid Aryat. When the army arrived, Abraha sent a letter to Aryat saying: "We share the same religion and homeland. We must behave in favour of the people of our religion and homeland. So, fight a duel with me if you wish. The triumphant one will be the king and will not kill the Abyssinian people who advocate the defeated one of us". Aryat agreed on the suggestion of Abraha. Yet, the latter intended to plot against Aryat. Abraha hid a slave near to the battlefield they would duel in. Aryat rushed to strike Abraha whose nose got split accordingly; for that he was then called Al Ashram. The latent slave got out and killed Aryat. So, Abraha decided to reward his slave by fulfilling whatever he wished. The latter expressed his wish saying: "No woman shall be married to her husband until I have sexual intercourse with her first". Abraha agreed. He continued doing so for a duration. Then, the people of Yemen attacked and killed him. So, Abraha said to them: "It is time to be free".

The news of the murder of Aryat reached Alnagashi. So, he decided to kill Abraha and seize his country. Yet, Abraha learnt about the decision of Alnagashi. So, he sent a letter to Alnagashi deluding him that: "Aryat was the one who had fought me first in order to weaken your kingship and murder your soldiers. So, I fought and defeated him. Yet, I am at your service". Consequently, Alnagashi became pleased with him and agreed on his deed.

The biographers said: When Alnagashi became pleased with Abraha, the latter built an unprecedented church. It was built with white, red, yellow and black marble, ornamented with gold and silver, surrounded by gemstones and was made special by a marvelous red ruby. It was scented with musk. Abraha called it Al Qullays (also spelled Al Qalis) and he sent a letter to Alnagashi informing him of its construction and that he intended to divert the Arabs to perform pilgrimage therein instead of Mecca.

When the Arabs talked about the letter of Abraha to Alnagashi, one of them became enraged. So, he went to that church and relieved himself therein. When Abraha knew about the behavior of that man and the reason behind it; that the church was not eligible for pilgrimage, he got furious and swore to proceed to the Sacred House (the Kaaba) to destroy it. Abraha had some Arab men, two of which were Mohammed ibn Khuzai Al Dhakwani and his brother Qays. Abraha appointed Mohammed as a ruler over the tribe of Mudhar and ordered him to call the people to perform pilgrimage around the church of Al Qullays that he had built.

Mohammed proceeded with his men until he reached the land of the tribe of Kinanah – while the people of Tuhama knew the reason for his coming. So, they sent a man belonging to the tribe of Hudhayl, who was called Urwa ibn Hiyad, and he threw an arrow to Mohammed which killed him. The latter's brother – Qays – fled and hastened to Abraha to tell him the news. Thus, Abraha fell into a rage and swore to raid the tribe of Kinanah and demolish the Kaaba. In this regard, he went forth along with the Abyssinians and a giant elephant. Upon knowing that, the Arabs saw that they should fight him. So, a noble man belonging to the people and kings of Yemen who was called Dhu Nafr went forth to fight Abraha defending the House of God, Exalted is He. When both parties met, Dhu Nafr along with his associated got defeated and captured. So, he said to Abraha: "O king, do not kill me may I help you". So, Abraha enchained him. When Abraha arrived at the land of Khatham, Nufail ibn Habib, followed by some Arab tribes, faced and fought him. Then, Abraha defeated and captured Nufail. The latter said to Abraha: "Do not kill me. I will be your guide in the land of the Arabs". So, Abraha enchained him. Then, Abraha passed by Al Taif where Masoud ibn Muattib at the head of some men of the tribe of Thaqif met him. They told him that they would send a guide with him. So, Abu Righal accompanied Abraha as his guide but he died when they reached Al Muhassar. Therefore, the Arabs threw stones at his grave and the subsequent people used to do so.

At Al Muhassar, Abraha sent an Abyssinian man named Al Aswad ibn Maqsoud riding a horse to Mecca. He seized the wealth of the people of Mecca, among which were two hundred camels possessed by Abd Al Muttalib – who was at that time the master of the tribe of Quraysh - to bring it to Abraha. Subsequently, the tribes of Quraysh, Kinanah and Hudhayl in addition to the people who were at the Sanctuary of Mecca (Al Haram) intended to fight him. Then, they realized that they had not enough capacity to do so. Thus, they gave up that idea.

Afterwards, Abraha sent Hinata Al Himyari to Mecca and instructed him to ask about the noblest and master of the tribe of Quraysh to tell him this message: "The King of Abyssinia tells you: 'I do not come to fight you. Rather, I come for destroying the Sacred House'; So, if you do not engage in war against him, he will not kill you". Abraha added to Hinata: "If their master does not intend to fight me, bring him to me".

When Hinata arrived at Mecca, he asked about the master of Quraysh. So, he was told that it was Abd Al Muttalib ibn Hashim ibn Abd Manaf. Hence, Hinata went to him and informed him of the message of Abraha. Abd Al Muttalib replied to him: "By God, we do not want to engage in war against him and we have not enough power to do so. This is the Sacred House of God and His Khalil (i.e. friend) Abraham. God only can defend His Sacred House and Sanctuary against Abraha if He wills. And if He lets Abraha do what he wants, by God we cannot defend the House".

Hinata said to Abd Al Muttalib: "Then, come with me to king Abraha; because he ordered me to do so". Hence, Abd Al Muttalib accompanied with some of his offspring went with Hinata. When they reached the gate of Abraha, Abd Al Muttalib asked the soldiers about his companion Dhu Nafr. They let him visit Dhu Nafr while he was in prison. Abd Al Muttalib asked him: "Do you have a poem concerning what we are experiencing?". Dhu Nafr replied to him: "How could a captive like me waiting for being murdered at any time say a poem? I can only enjoin my companion Onays, the Elephant handler, to corroborate you before the king and get his permission to let you ask him for whatever you want".

Accordingly, Onays said to Abraha: "O king, the master of the tribe of Quraysh is at your gate. Let him in and do good to him". So, Abraha allowed Abd Al Muttalib to come in and honored him when he admired the smart, great appearance of the latter. Abraha came down from his throne and sat on his carpet and let Abd Al Muttalib sit beside him. Then, Abraha said to his interpreter to ask Abd Al Muttalib for what he wanted. So, Abd Al Muttalib replied that he wanted the king to give him back his two hundred camels. Then, Abraha replied to him through the interpreter: "I admired you once I saw you but now I am displeased with you when I heard your words. You want your camels which I have seized and do not care about the House, even though it is your religion and the religion of your forefathers, which I have come to destroy!". So, Abd Al Muttalib replied to him: "I am the owner of the camels whereas the House has a Lord who will defend it". However, Abraha challenged that he could destroy the House.

When Abraha returned the camels to Abd Al Muttalib, the latter went back to the tribe of Quraysh and told them about the intention of Abraha to destroy the Kaaba. He also ordered them to leave Mecca to the paths of the mountains for fearing to be harmed by the army. Then, Abd Al Muttalib took hold of the door knocker of the Kaaba. He as well as some people of the tribe of Quraysh supplicated God to advocate them against Abraha and his troopers. Abd Al Muttalib said:

O my Lord, I know that You alone can defeat them.. So, protect Your Sacred House from them.

Your enemy is the enemy of the House.. Prevent them from ruining Your House.

Afterwards, Abd Al Muttalib let the door knocker and went forth to the paths of the mountains seeking refuge from Abraha and waiting for what he would do. In the morning, Abraha prepared his giant, unparalleled elephant and mobilized his army to head to Mecca. When they directed the elephant to Mecca, it knelt down. The troopers hit the elephant to force it to move forward but it refused. On the contrary, the elephant moved so easily whenever it was directed towards Yemen, the Levant or the Orient; i.e. towards any other direction other than Mecca. Suddenly and rapidly, God, the Almighty and Sublime, sent upon Abraha and his army flocks of birds from the seaside that looked like hooks. Each bird held three stones, one in its beak and one in each foot. The stones were as small as chickpeas and lentils. Anyone of the troopers that was hit by a stone got immediately killed. Only a few of them remained alive. So, they fled asking about Nufail to guide them to the way of return to Yemen. Yet, Nufail abstained from guiding them after seeing the punishment of God for them.

Then, they retreated from Mecca and some of which fell on the way and died. Abraha suffered severe injuries till the remnants arrived with him at Sanaa. He died there. It was claimed that his organs fell off one after the other and his heart burst from his chest.

The biographers said: When Abraha – the Christian king in Abyssinia - perished, his son Yaksum came to the reign. So, the tribes of Himyar and Yemen were humiliated and the Abyssinians conquered them. Then, Yaksum died and his brother Masrouq ibn Abraha reigned. The kingship of the Abyssinians over Yemen, since Aryat entered there till the Persian killed Masrouq and ex-pelled the Abyssinians from Yemen, continued for seventy two years. During this epoch, four Abyssinian kings reigned: Aryat, then Abraha, then Yaksum, then Masrouq. Later on, Sayf ibn Dhu Yazan Al Himyari, nicknamed Abu Murra, headed to Caesar – the king of Rome – to complain to him of the Abyssinians and ask him to expel them from Yemen and appoint whoever he wished from among the Romans as a king over Yemen. Nevertheless, Caesar did not respond to his request. So, Sayf went to Al Hirah to meet its ruler, Alnoaman ibn Almundhir, appointed by Khosrow (the king of Persia) over Al Hirah and the lands of Iraq beyond it. He complained to Alnoaman the affliction and humiliation they suffered. Alnoaman asked Sayf to accompany him upon his visit to Khosrow.

When Sayf ibn Dhu Yazan was allowed to come in to Khosrow, he complained to him that the Abyssinians raided his country, Yemen, and sought his help, asking him to rule Yemen as he was better than the Abyssinians. Yet, Khosrow refused justifying so by saying: "Yemen is far from our land. Moreover, it lacks prosperity. Rather, it has cattle and camels which we are in no need of. I would not let a Persian army engage in a war in the land of the Arabs. This will be of no benefit for me".

Afterwards, Khosrow gave Sayf ten thousand dirhams and nice garments. However, Sayf let the money for the people. So, boys, slaves and maids took it. When Khosrow was informed of that, he ordered his men to bring Sayf to him. When Sayf came in, Khosrow told him astonishingly: "You gave up the money I had granted you to the public!". Sayf replied to him: "What can I do with money! The mountains of my land, Yemen, are full of gold and silver". Sayf tried to make Yemen desirable for Khosrow when he found that he had no interest therein. Sayf proceeded his words: "I came to the king seeking his refuge against injustice and humility". So, Khosrow said to him: "Dwell in my kingdom till I consider your matter". So Sayf did.

Khosrow held a meeting with the persons whom he used to ask for their opinion. So, one of them suggested: "O king, you can send with Sayf to Yemen the imprisoned men whom you intend to kill. If they perish, it will be in your interest. If they conquer Yemen, it will be added to your kingship". Khosrow agreed on this opinion. He ordered his soldiers to count the imprisoned men. They found eight hundred men in prison. So, he said: "Appoint the man who belongs to the best lineage as their leader". They appointed a man called Wahrez (also spelled Vahrez). They went forth with Sayf ibn Dhu Yazan embarking eight ships. Two of which drowned with its people. So, their number became six hundred men. Wahrez asked Sayf about what kind of support he could give. Sayf told him that he would support him with Arab men and knights. Moreover, he would accompany him till death or victory. Wahrez said to him: "You are fair".

Thus, Sayf mobilized as much men as he could. Masrouq ibn Abraha heard about that news. Therefore, the latter mobilized his Abyssinian troops. He headed towards them till the two armies approached each other. Wahrez sent his son Nawzadh at the head of some knights to find out the way of their fight.

When Nawzadh faced them, they murdered him. Wahrez accordingly got so enraged at them. So, he ordered his troops to show him the Abyssinian king. They did and he said to them: "I will throw an arrow at the king. If his associates do not move, this means I have missed the target. So, do not move till I give you a permission. On the contrary, if you see his associates look back and surround him, this means that my arrow has hit the target. So, attack them".

Then, Wahrez throw his arrow at the Abyssinian king and he was killed immediately. The Abyssinians looked back, so the Persians attacked and defeated them. Some of the Abyssinians were killed and others fled. Hence, Wahrez headed to enter Sanaa but he demolished its gate first in order to enter there raising his banner.

When Wahrez seized Yemen and freed it from the Abyssinians, he sent a letter to Khosrow telling him about that news and sent the funds to him. Then, Khosrow replied to him in a letter ordering him to appoint Sayf ibn Dhu Yazan as the king of Yemen. Besides, Khosrow imposed on Sayf ibn Dhu Yazan a poll tax (jizyah) and a land tax to pay annually. Khosrow then sent a letter to Wahrez ordering him to come back to Persia. Dhu Yazan – the father of Sayf – was one of the kings of Yemen.

On the other hand, it was said that Dhu Yazan was the one who came to Khosrow seeking his help but he died at his gate. So, his son Sayf came to Khosrow telling him: "I am the son of the Yemeni elder man whom you promised of vanquishing the Abyssinians and he died at your kingdom. So, Khosrow sympathized with Sayf and supported him by the way mentioned above.

Ibn Hisham ibn Mohammed said: When the ships of the Persians appeared, Masrouq – the Abyssinian king – went forth to them at the head of one hundred thousand army composing of the Abyssinians, Himyarites and Bedouins (Arabs of the desert). A lot of people followed ibn Dhu Yazan. The latter was led by Wahrez. When Masrouq saw that his enemies were a few, he disdained them and became self-deceived. He sent to Wahzer telling him: "How dare you come with this few army to face my huge army! You as well as your associates are naïve. So, I will let you retreat if you wish. Otherwise, we can fight one another or grant you a respite to consider your matter". Wahrez replied to him: "Grant me a respite". So, Masrouq did.

After the first ten days of the respite, the son of Wahrez went forth till he approached the army of the enemy. Then, they killed him. So, when only one day lasted before the respite came to an end, Wahrez ordered to fire the ships and clothes of his own army. He let only the clothes they were wearing. Besides, he let them eat and he threw the remnant food with them in the sea. Then, he justified to them his deeds saying: "I fired your ships to know that you cannot turn back to your country. As for your clothes that I fired, this is because I do not want them to be seized by the enemy if we are defeated. As for the food I threw in the sea, this is for letting none of you wish to live one day with this food. If you will support me in fighting and be patient, inform me of that. Otherwise, I will depend on my own sword till I may be killed but I will not enable them of killing me". They replied to him: "We will support you in fighting till we all die or vanquish". In the morning, Wahrez mobilized his associates and repeated to them: "Either you vanquish or you die honorably". Further, he threw an arrow at the Abyssinian king killing him. So, Wahrez defeated the Abyssinians, captured a great deal of spoils from them and seized Sanaa as well as the other cities of Yemen.

Ibn Isaac said: When Wahrez turned back to Khosrow, having appointed Sayf as the king of Yemen, he raided Abyssinia. He killed a lot of the Abyssinians except a few humble remnants which he held as slaves. Then, an Abyssinian man corrupted Yemen. When this news reached Khosrow, he sent Wahrez to Yemen at the head of four thousand Persians. He ordered him to kill all the Abyssinians and Sudaneses he would find in Yemen. So, he did and dwelled there, levying taxes to Khosrow, till he died.

After Wahrez had died, Khosrow sent a leader called Zain to Yemen to rule it. However, the latter was an oppressive and a transgressor ruler. Therefore, Khosrow ousted him and appointed Marzbān ibn Wahrez instead. When the latter died, Khosrow appointed his son Bīnagār ibn Marzbān as the new king of Yemen. After the latter had died, Khosrow appointed Khurra Khusraw as the king.

Yet, when Khosrow became angry with Khurra Khusraw, he swore that the Yemeni people should bring Khurra Khusraw humiliated to him. So, they did. When they arrived, a noble Persian man received him and gave him a sword belonging to the father of Khosrow. So, Khosrow did not kill Khurra Khusraw but only ousted him. Then, Khosrow appointed Badhan (also spelled Badham) as the king of Yemen. He ruled it till God, the Almighty and Sublime, sent Prophet Mohammed (PBUH) to mankind.

The biographers said: There was a truce between Khosrow Anushiruwan and the king of Rome, Justinianus (also spelled Justinian). Later on, a hostility arose between a leader, appointed by the Roman king, called Khalid ibn Jabala and a leader, appointed by Khosrow, called Almundhir ibn Alnoaman. So, Khalid invaded the region of Almundhir, killed a great number of the latter's associates and captured funds. Therefore, Almundhir complained to Khosrow. Thus, Khosrow sent a letter to the king of Rome reminding him of the peace treaty held between both of them and telling him about what was faced by Almundhir whom he (Khosrow) had appointed as a ruler. Besides, Khosrow asked the king of Rome to make Khalid render the spoils he captured from the region of Almundhir and pay a blood money (Diyah) for whom he murdered. Finally, he warned him not to neglect his letter for that would be a breach of the peace treaty held between both of them.

Then, Khosrow continued to send letters frequently to the king of Rome regarding that matter whereas the latter did not care about those letters at all. Consequently, Khosrow raided him at the head of more than ninety thousand troopers. So, he seized the cities of Dara, Osroene, Qinnasrin, Aleppo, Homs, Antakya – which was the best city in the Levant – and a lot of cities. He captured the spoils there. He also captured the people of Antakya and moved them into the land of Al Sawad. The king of Rome was paying him a land tax. Kavad I had previously ordered in the final days of his reign to perform a land survey – on the even as well as the uneven ground - in order to impose the suitable land tax. So, the survey began to be performed but Kavad I perished before the survey was completed. When Khosrow came to the reign, he ordered to complete the land survey and count the date palms and olives therein. Then, he sought the opinion of the people with regard to gathering the land tax to put it in the Public treasury to make use of these funds for cultivation. They agreed upon imposing the land tax on the foods which sustained the people and beasts; wheat, barley, rice, grapevines, date palms and olives. So, they imposed seven dirhams on each patch of land containing fresh dates, one dirham on each four Persian date palms, one dirham on each six worst date palms and one dirham on each six olive trees. They imposed the land tax on the date palms existing within a garden, other than the ones outside. They imposed the poll tax on the people except the great men of the state, the members of noble houses troopers, writers and servants of the king. They made the poll tax different; twelve, eight, six or four dirhams, according to the financial position of a subject. The poll tax was not imposed on the people under the age of twenty years nor those above the age of fifty years. Umar ibn Al Khattab (May God be pleased with him) followed this rule.

Among the events that took place during the era of Khosrow Anushiruwan was that he became angry with his minister Bozorg-mehr. So, Khowrow arrested him in a place that looked like a grave. He enchained him, dressed him in rough wool garments, provided him with only two bread loaves and crushed salt to eat and a beaker of water. Khosrow ordered his soldiers to inform him with every word Bozorgmehr would utter. However, Bozorg-mehr was saying nothing for months. So, Anushiruwan said to his soldiers: "Let his companions visit him and order them to share talk with him, then inform me of what he would talk about".

A group of his intimate companions visited him and said: "O' wise man, we see your appearance and health unchanged even though you are enchained and experience distress! He said to them: "There are six humors that compose the human body. So, I experience one of them every day. This is what keeps my status steady like that". They said: "Tell us about these humors".

He said: The first humor was: Trusting God, the Almighty and Sublime. Secondly: Knowing that fate is inevitable. Thirdly: Being patient is the best means for the afflicted person. Fourthly:

There is no action that I can do other than to be patient and I did not get alarmed. Fifthly: There may be worse misfortune than that I suffer now. Sixthly: Distress will be driven away by relief in a short while. Later, Khosrow Anushiruwan killed Bozorgmehr.

Bozorgmehr was sage. Among his wise quotes: "If there is something better than life, then it is health. If there is something similar to health, it is sufficiency. If there is something over death, it is ailment. If there is something similar to ailment, it is poverty". There were four notes he had listed: "Firstly: If God is the Most Sublime one, then knowing Him is the greatest field of knowledge. Secondly: If sustenance is already assigned by God, then being stingy is useless. Thirdly: If matters are run by the decree and will of God, then our calamities do not take place except for certain causes regardless of being known or unknown to us. Fourthly: If Man has a various composition, then it is impossible to seek a steady status for him".

Regarding rationality, Bozorgmehr said: "Consideration is the best evidence of rationality". In addition, he said: A reasonable one shall be like a person passing by a river. Another quote of Bozorgmehr was: "Being lenient towards people is half of reason". Moreover, he said: "A reasonable one should not dwell in a country free from five things: a strict ruler, a fair judge, a prosperous market, a running river and an efficient doctor".

He also added concerning rationality: "Intellect is the best thing granted to Man. If he is deprived of it, he should commit himself to silence. If he is deprived of the capability to do so, then death would be a better protection for him". He was asked: "Which ones are better than the others: the wealthy or the scholars?". He said: "The scholars are better than the wealthy". So, he was asked: "Then, why do the scholars seek the wealthy more frequently than the latter do? He replied to this: "Because the scholars know well the superiority of wealth whereas the wealthy ignore the superiority of knowledge".

During the era of Khosrow Anushiruwan was Imru Al Qays ibn Hajar (Hujr) ibn Al Harith ibn Amr Al Kindi. He said in his poems that he left urban regions and that he belonged to the people of Najd. He depicted in his poetry the dwellings of the tribe of Asad. Kavad I had appointed Al Harith ibn Amr as the king of the Arabs. So, the latter appointed his son Hajar as the leader of the tribe of Asad. Hajar used to impose a certain amount of tax on the people of the tribe. When they abstained from paying, he went forth to them, seized their funds and killed them with staffs. So, they were called the slaves of the staff. He also captured a faction of them amongst which was Ubaid ibn Al Abras. Then, he set them free and let them turn back to their homeland.

Afterwards, Anushiruwan came to the reign and appointed Al-noaman ibn Maa Al Samaa. Al Harith fled accordingly, pursued by the knights of Almundhir but they did not manage to catch him. However, they caught his son Amr and killed him. Then, they killed Hajar who had before expelled his son Imru Al Qays because he aggressed against some women to give him the woman he loved. So, when his father knew that, he ordered a servant to "kill Imru Al Qays and bring me his two eyes". The servant slaughtered a sheep and brought its eyes to Hajar who in turn regretted killing his son. Subsequently, the servant confessed to him that he did not kill Imru Al Qays. Hajar ordered him to bring his son. So, he rendered his son to him and Hajar commanded him to give up poetry. Then, Hajar expelled his son again because of his disobedience.

When Imru Al Qays knew about the murder of his father, he decided not to eat meat-based food till he took revenge for his father's death. He went out to Caesar to advocate him. Then, the daughter of Caesar loved him, so, he used to meet her. Yet, Al Tammah ibn Qays Al Asdi, whose father had been killed by Hajar, knew that. So, he ratted Imru Al Qays out to Caesar. Subsequently, Imru Al Qays fled but Caesar ordered to pursue him. So, he was killed near Ankara. His mother died during his cradle days.

It was reported that some people came from Yemen to meet Messenger Mohammed (PBUH) but they missed their way and needed water. Meanwhile, a caravan was passing by, so one of them recited some poetic verses concerning their need of water. They said that Imru Al Qays was the one who said those verses. Then, the Yemeni people moved forward and found palatable water from which they drank, otherwise they would be perished. When they reached the Messenger of God (PBUH), they said to him: "God gave us life by two poetic verses of Imru Al Qays". The Messenger (PBUH) said to them: "Imru Al Qays is the leader of the poets into the Hell".

It was reported that the earliest poems were not but little verses recited by a man when he faced a challenge. Then, the first one to introduce extraordinary meanings and erotic poetry was Imru Al Qays.

Khosrow had sons, so he made his son Hormizd succeed him...

CHAPTER 6

Number of prophets and messengers

It is said that number of prophets are 124000 and there were 313 messengers; first one of them was Adam; four prophets were Syrians, Adam, Seth, Idris and Noah; Four prophets were Arabs, Hud, Shu'ayb, Saleh and Mohammed; the first prophet of Banu Israel was Moses; and the first of messengers was Adam and the last one was Mohammed.

It is said that there were 104 books were revealed by God. 50 books were revealed to Seth, 30 books were revealed to Idris; 10 books were revealed to Abraham; there were 10 books were revealed to Moses before Torah; then Torah, Gospel, Psalms and Quran.

Books of Abraham were examples but the books of Moses were lessons.

It is said that messengers are 315 ones. Some scholars said that they are 8000 prophets, 4000 ones from them were for Banu Israel.

It is said that books of Abraham were revealed on the first day of Ramadan, Torah was revealed on 6th of Ramadan, and Psalms was revealed on 12th of Ramadan. Also, Gospel was revealed on 10th of Ramadan, but Quran was revealed on 24th of Ramadan.

Tale of virtue of this nation

Bahz bin Hakim narrated according to his father, and his grandfather that he heard the Prophet (PBUH) saying about God, Most High saying: "You are the best of peoples ever raised up for mankind. He said: 'You are the completion of seventy nations, you are the best of them, and the most honorable of them to God."

Tale of years' number among prophets

Ibn 'Abbas said that 1200 years passed from the time of Adam till Noah; 1143 years passed from the time of Noah till Abraham; 575 years passed from the time of Abraham till Moses; 579 years passed from the time of Moses till David; 1053 years passed from the time of David till Jesus and 600 years passed from the time of Jesus to Mohammed (PBUH).

Ibn Isaac said 1200 years passed from the time of Adam till Noah; 1142 years passed from the time of Noah till Abraham; 565

years passed from the time of Abraham till Moses; 569 years passed from the time of Moses till David; 1356 years passed from the time of David till Jesus and 600 years passed from the time of Jesus to Mohammed (PBUH).

A scholar said that 5800 years passed from the creation of Adam until sending the Prophet (PBUH).

Tale of the prophets' professions

Ibn 'Abbas said that Adam was a farmer, Noah was a carpenter, Idris was a tailor, Abraham was a farmer, Shu'ayb was a shepherd, Moses was a shepherd, David was a blacksmith, Solomon was a king, Jesus was not saving for tomorrow, Mohammed (PBUH) was a shepherd and Eve was working on hand knitting to cloth herself and children.

Tale of the circumcised messengers

Author said: Adam was created circumcised, Seth, Idris, Noah, Sam, Hud, Saleh, the prophet of Companions of the Well, Lot, Joseph, Moses, Shu'ayb, Solomon, Zachariah, Jesus and our Prophet (PBUH) were born circumcised but Abraham was tested with circumcision..

Tale of some ancient peoples

One of them was Khalid ibn Snan Al'absi

It was narrated that he was one of the prophets.

It was narrated that there was a fire emerged in the desert between Mecca and Medina, some Arab sects were worshipping it, a man said he was from 'Abs called Khalid ibn Snan Al'absi who distinguished it. He said to his brothers that he would die and "when I die, bury me in that place, after a year, watch my grave if you saw a tailless donkey, kill it and excavate my grave, I would talk to you about everything would happen."

He died, they buried him and they watched his grave after a year and the tailless donkey came and they killed it, when they were about to excavate his grave, his brothers said if we excavated it, it would be shameful for us and so they did not.

When the Prophet (PBUH) was sent, daughter of Khalid ibn Snan went to the Prophet (PBUH) after migration and told him that she was the daughter of Khalid ibn Snan, it was said that the Prophet (PBUH) welcomed her and said that her father was a prophet and his people missed him and he told them his story and said if their people excavated his grave, he would tell them about the position of that nation and me.

Another man was Gergees

He was a righteous man who lived during the age of some of the disciples of Jesus (PBUH).

It was said that there was a tyrant king ruling Mosul and Gergees was a righteous man from the people of Palestine who concealed his faith together with a band of people who lived during the age of some of the disciples of Jesus (PBUH); He had much money and he was always giving alms. King of Mosul set an idol, set a fire and showed that to people, he said to them that who would not prostrate for that idol, would be thrown in the fire. Gergees said to him "I knew that you were a servant who do not cause harm for yourself or others but God is who possesses you and all creatures. You made an idol that does not hear nor see and made it temptation for people." The king ordered that Gergees shall be tortured till death but he did not die, he asked Gergees "do not you feel the pain of that torture?", he said "no, as my God protects me, so you fear that torture". The king put him in prison, God sent to him an angel to set him free and told him to fight against his enemy and be patient 'You will be killed for four times, and in every time I will get back your soul to you'. The king caught him and killed him for four times but in every time he was given life again. The queen and 34,000 people believed in him, then he was killed and died for ever.

Another righteous man was Shamshoon

It is said that he was one of the righteous people who lived in a village among Romans. His people was worshipping idols; he was conquering them and standing against them. They went to his wife and tempted her to chain him. She tried a lot but she failed as he was very powerful. Once she managed to know how to chain him, she sent to her people who took him cutting his nose and ears and scoop out his eyes. They chained him before the people. He supplicated to God to give him power to dominate them, he took two pillars of the city where people and the king watching him and pulled them, destroying the whole city with its people.

Others were companions of the cave

They were people who fled from their king when he asked them to worship idols. They went to a cave and three hundred years later, unknowingly, a man among them went to the city to buy them their needs. The king knew about them and went to the cave and blocked its entrance. God caused them to die-like while sleeping. Then, God inspired someone from the people of this village to destroy that wall that was blocking the cave, they awake and looked at each other and said to one of them who was responsible for buying their stuff to buy food for them. He found that the city and the people were changed, when he was about to pay the price of what he bought, people discovered engraved coins and thought he found a treasure, at the end, he told them about his story where they fled yesterday from the king who wanted to make them worship idols to a cave and that they slept and when they waked up, they got out to buy some food. People went with the man to the cave and they believed that God made them asleep and resurrected them again to be a sign for people to worship God. Then, they slept and their souls were seized in the cave and God prevented people to reach them and no one could get in the cave and the king built a mosque in front of the cave and chose that day as a feast for them.

Others were companions of the trench

They were those people for whom the trenches were dug and fired, then they were thrown in them.

Scholars differed regarding the reason behind that, some of them said that they were people enforced to polytheism and they refused.

Some scholars said that their king had sexual intercourse with his sister and wanted people to do like him but they refused.

Suhaib reported that God's Messenger (PBUH) saying: "There lived a king before you and he had a (court) magician. As the magician grew old, he said to the king: I have grown old, send some young boy to me so that I should teach him magic. The king sent to him a young man so that he can train him in magic. And on his way, the young man found a monk sitting there. The young man listened to the monk's talk and was impressed by it. It became his habit that on his way to the magician he met the monk and set there and he came to the magician late. The magician beat him because of delay. He made a complaint of that to the monk and he said to him: When you feel afraid of the magician, say: Members of my family had detained me. And when you feel afraid of your family you should say: The magician had detained me. It so happened that there came a huge beast of prey and it blocked the way of the people, and the young boy said: I will come to know today whether the magician is superior or the monk is superior. He picked up a stone and said: O God, if the affair of the monk is dearer to Thee than the affair of the magician, cause death to this animal so that the people should be able to move about freely. He threw that stone towards it and killed it and the people began to move about on the path freely. The young man then came to that monk and informed him and the monk said: Son, today you are superior to me. Your affair has come to a stage where I find that you would be soon put to a trial, and in case you are put to a trial, don't give my clue. That young man began to treat the blind and those suffering from leprosy and he in fact began to cure people from all kinds of illness. When a companion of the king who had gone blind heard about that man, he came to him, presenting numerous gifts and said: If you cure me, all these things collected together here would be yours. He said: I myself do not cure anyone.

It is God Who cures and if you affirm faith in God, I shall also supplicate God to cure you. He affirmed his faith in God and God cured him and he came to the king and sat by his side as he used to sit before. The king said to him: Who restored your eyesight? He said: My Lord. Thereupon he said: It means that your Lord is One besides me. He said: My Lord and your Lord is God, so the king took hold of him and tormented him till he gave a clue of that boy. The young man was thus summoned and the king said to him: O boy, it has been conveyed to me that you have become so much proficient in your magic that you cure the blind and those suffering from leprosy. Thereupon he said: I do not cure anyone; it is God Who cures. They argued against each other regarding the one who cures.

The king imprisoned him and began to torture him. So he gave a clue of the monk. The monk was thus called and it was said to him: You should abandon your religion. He refused to do so. He ordered for a saw to be brought and when it was done, the king placed it in the middle of his head and tore it into parts till a part fell down. Then the courtier of the king was brought and it was said to him: Abandon your religion. He also refused to do so, and the saw was placed in the midst of his head and it was torn till a part fell down. Then that young boy was brought and it was said to him: Abandon your religion. He refused to do so and he was handed over to a group of his courtiers. And he said to them: Take him to such mountain; make him climb up that mountain and when you reach its top, ask him to abandon his faith, but if he refuses to do so, then throw him down the mountain. So they took him and made him climb up the mountain and he said: O God, save me from them in any way You like and the mountain began to quake and they all fell down and that person came walking to the king. The king said to him: What has happened to my courtiers?

He said: God has saved me from them. He again handed him to some of his courtiers and said: Carry him in a small boat and when you reach the middle of the ocean, ask him to renounce his religion, but if he does not renounce his religion throw him (into the water). So they took him and he said: O God, save me. Then the boat turned over and they were drowned and he came walking to the king.

He entered to the king, the king said to him: What has happened to courtiers? He said: God saved me from them, and he said to the king: You cannot kill me until you do what I ask you to do. And he said: What is that? The man replied: You should gather people in a plain and hang me by the trunk of a tree. Then grab an arrow from the quiver and say: In the name of God, the Lord of the young boy; then shoot an arrow and if you do that, then you would be able to kill me. So the king called the people in an open plain and tied the boy to the trunk of a tree, then he grabbed an arrow from his quiver and then placed the arrow in the bow and then said: In the name of God, the Lord of the young boy; he then shot an arrow and it bit his temple. The boy placed his hands upon the temple where the arrow had bit him and he died and the people said: We affirm our faith in the Lord of this young man. The courtiers came to the king and it was said to him: Do you see that God has actually done what you aimed at averting. The people have affirmed their faith in the Lord. The king commanded ditches to be dug at important points in the path. When these ditches were dug, and the fire was set in them, it was said to the people: who would not turn back from the boy's religion, would be thrown in the fire. A woman came with her child and she felt hesitant in jumping into the fire and the child said to her: "O mother, endure this ordeal for it is the Truth."

One of them was Juraij, the worshipper.

Abu Hurairah reported the Messenger saying: "Three people talked in cradle, Jesus; the son of the shepherd and…"

There was a prostitute who had been a beauty incarnate. She said to the people: If you like I can allure him to evil. She offered herself to him but he is not interested in her. She came to a shepherd who lived near the temple and she offered herself to him, accordingly he had a sexual intercourse with her and so she became pregnant, but when she gave birth to a child she claimed that this baby is from Juraij. So they came and asked him to go out, they destroyed the temple and began to beat him. He said: What is the matter? They said: You have committed fornication with this prostitute and she has given birth to a child. He said: Where is the child? They brought the child and he said: just leave me so that I should perform prayer. And he performed prayer and when he finished, he came to the child. He hit his stomach and said: O boy, tell us who is your father? the baby said: He is the shepherd. So people turned towards Juraij, apologized to him and asking him to grant them blessing and said: We will construct your temple again but with gold. He refused saying. No, just rebuild it with mud as it had been, and they did that.

Then there was a baby who was sucking his mother's breast when a person dressed in fine garment came riding upon a beast.

His mother said: O God, make my child like this one. the baby left sucking and began to look towards him, and said: O God, don't make me like him. He then returned to the breast of her mother and began to suck the milk. (Abu Huraira) said: I perceived as if I am seeing God's Messenger (PBUH) as he is explaining the scene of his sucking milk with his forefinger in his mouth and sucking that. Abu Huraira further reported God's Apostle saying: then a girl happened to pass by him who was being beaten, his mother said: O God, don't make my child like her.

He left sucking the milk, and looked towards her saying: O God, make me like her, and there was a talk between them. His mother said: I said: O God, make my child like him, and you said: O God, don't make me like him, and when the girl passed by and she was beaten I said: O God, don't make my child like her, and you said: O God, make me like her. Thereupon he said: That man on the beast was a tyrant, and I said: O God, don't make me like him, and they were falsely accusing her that she committed fornication whereas in fact she had not committed and that she committed theft whereas she had not committed theft, so I said: O God, make me like her."

One of them was Barsisa

It is said that he is a monk from Banu Israel, the Satan affected a girl and made their family to think that her cure was at the monk. They went to the monk to cure her but he refused. They insisted on taking her till he accepted her and when they met, the Satan whispered to him till he had sexual intercourse with her. The Satan came to him and said kill her and when her family came, tell them that she died and you buried her; the monk did. The Satan went to her family and said to them that the monk made her pregnant and killed her, and then he buried her.

Her family came to the monk and asked him about her he said to them that she died and he buried her. They took the monk to punish him, meanwhile, the Satan came to him and said if you prostrated to me twice, I would make them let you go. He did. It is thought that he is the one about whom God Exalted is He says: " [The hypocrites are] like the example of Satan when he says to man, "Disbelieve." But when he disbelieves, he says, "Indeed, I am disassociated from you. Indeed, I fear God, Lord of the worlds "كَمَثَلِ الشَّيْطَانِ إِذْ قَالَ لِلْإِنسَانِ اكْفُرْ فَلَمَّا كَفَرَ قَالَ إِنِّي بَرِيءٌ مِّنكَ إِنِّي أَخَافُ اللَّـهَ ". "رَبَّ الْعَالَمِينَ (59:16).

Tale of Sheba

Scholars said that when Balqis (Queen of Sheba) ruled her people, they used to fight against each other about their valley. She used to prohibit them but they did not obey her. Then, she denounced the rule and left them fighting and when the evil increased among them, they repented. They went to her and insisted that she had to rule them again, she agreed upon a condition to obey her. They said we would obey you. She went to their valley where the flood came to it from a distance of three days. She commanded them to build a dam between the two mountains where it blocked the water behind and made gates for it till they got water equally. They had two gardens; one on the right and the other on the left. The land became very fertilized and their fruits were increased. It was said to them: "Eat from the provisions of your Lord and be grateful to Him." That city had 13 villages and God sent to them 13 prophets to their people but they disbelieved them and turned away refusing, so the flood of the dam was sent to them, and God replaced their two fields of gardens with gardens of bitter fruit. God sent them a rat that dug under the dam and drowned their gardens and became infertile. Yet they said, "Our Lord, lengthen the distance between our journeys," and wronged themselves, so God made them narrations and dispersed them. Indeed in that are signs for everyone who is patient and grateful.

Tale of San'a

Scholars said that there was a man in Yemen, he was a believer, after the time of Jesus (PBUH), he had a garden; he was taking the food of his day and giving the rest as alms. He had three children, and when he died, they said that the property was little and the children were many; our father did that because the children were few and the property was much, so they insisted not to give the poor people and they decided that they would go out to collect their crops at early morning before people got up. So there came upon the garden an affliction from the Lord while they were asleep. God sent to them a fire that burnt their garden. So they set out, while lowering their voices: "There will surely not enter it today upon you [any] poor person." But when they saw it, they said, "Indeed, we are lost", then they perceived that it was a punishment from God and said: "Rather, we have been deprived". They said, "Exalted is our Lord! Indeed, we were wrongdoers." Then they approached one another, blaming each other. They said, "O woe to us; indeed we were transgressors".

Also, People of Grotto

Ibn `Umar narrated that God's Messenger (PBUH) said, "While three persons were traveling, they were overtaken by rain and they took shelter in a cave in a mountain. A big rock fell from the mountain over the mouth of the cave and blocked it. They said to each other. 'Think of such good and righteous deeds which, you did for God's sake only, and invoke God by giving reference to those deeds so that God may relieve you from your difficulty.

One of them said, 'O God! I had my parents who were very old and I had small children for whose sake I used to work as a shepherd. When I returned home at night after milking the sheep, I used to start giving the milk to my parents first and before giving it to my children. One day I went far away searching for a grazing place and did not return home till late at night and found that my parents had slept. I milked my sheep as usual then I brought the milk container and approached then, and I did not want to wake them up, and I also did not want to give the milk to my children before my parents though my children were crying, out of hunger, down at my feet, So this was the case till dawn. O God, if You considered that I had done that only for seeking Your pleasure, then kindly make us there an opening through which we can look at the sky.' So God made for them an opening for such purpose.

Then the second person said, 'O God! I had a she-cousin whom I ardently loved. I tried to seduce her but she refused till I paid her one-hundred Dinars So I worked hard till I collected one hundred Dinars and went to her with that, but when I approached her to have sexual intercourse with her, she said, 'O God's slave! Be afraid of God! Do not deflower me but legally, upon marriage. So I left her. O God, if You deem that I had done that only for seeking

Your pleasure, then please let the rock move to have a wider opening.' So God moved that rock to make the opening larger.

And the third person said 'O God, I employed a laborer for wages equal to a certain measure of rice, and when he had finished his job he demanded his wages, but when I presented his dues to him, he gave it up and refused to take it. Then I kept on sowing that rice for him (several times) till managed to buy with the price of the yield, some cows. Later on the laborer came to me and said. '(O God's slave!) Be afraid of God, and do not be unjust to me, give me my dues.' I said to him. 'Go and take those cows and their shepherd. So he took them and went. So, O God, If You considered that I had done so for seeking Your pleasure, then I hope that You will remove the remaining part of the rock.' And so God freed them from their difficulty.

Some of them is Alkifl

Ibn 'Umar said: "I heard the Prophet (PBUH) narrating a hadith, not just once or twice, even seven times, but I heard him saying it more than that. I heard him saying: 'There was a man called Alkifl among the children of Israel who did not restrain himself from committing sins. A woman came to him and he gave her sixty Dinars so he could sleep with her. When he sat up from her, as a man sits up from a woman, she began to tremble and cry, so he said: "Why are you crying, did I do something to harm you?" She said: "No. But it is because of what I did, I only did so out of need." He said: "You did this without having done it before, so leave me, and the money is for you." And then he said: "By God! I will never disobey You after that." He died during the night and morning came with: "Indeed God has forgiven Alkifl" written upon his door."

Tale of the leper, the bald and the blind

Abu Huraira, narrated that he heard God's Messenger (PBUH) saying:

There were three persons in Banu Israel, one was suffering from leprosy, the other was bald-headed and the third one was blind. God decided to test them. So, He sent an angel who came to the one who was suffering from leprosy and said: Which thing do you like most? He said: Beautiful color and fine skin, I wish for removal of that which makes me detestable in the eye of people. He wiped him and his illness was no more here and he was conferred upon beautiful color and beautiful skin.

The angel again said: Which property does you like most? He said: Camels or Cow (the narrator is, however, doubtful about it), but, out of the persons suffering from leprosy or baldness one of them definitely said: The camel. And the other one said: Cow. The one who demanded camel was bestowed upon a she-camel, in an advanced stage of pregnancy, and upon giving it, he said: May God bless you with this.

Then he came to the bald-headed person and said: Which thing do you like most? He said: Beautiful hair and that this baldness may be removed from me because of which people hate me. He wiped his body and his illness was removed and he was bestowed upon beautiful hair, and the angel said: Which wealth do you like most? He said: The cow. And he was given a pregnant cow and while handing it over to him, the angel said: May God bless you with this.

Then he came to the blind man and he said: Which thing do you like most? He said: God may restore my eyesight so that I can be able to see people with the help of that. He wiped his body and God restored to him his eyesight, and he (the angel) also said: Which wealth do you like most? He said: The flock of sheep. And he was given a pregnant goat.

It gave birth to young ones and it was happened that one's valley abounded in camels and the second one in cows and the third one in sheep. He then came to the one who had suffered from leprosy in his old form and shape and said: I am a poor person and my provision has run short in my journey and I cannot reach my destination except with the help of God and your favor. I beg you in His name Who gave you fine color and fine skin, and the camel in the shape of wealth, to confer upon me a camel which should carry me in my journey. He said: I have many responsibilities. Thereupon he said: I perceive as if I recognize you. Were you not suffering from leprosy whom people hated and you were a needy and God conferred upon you wealth? He said: I have inherited this property from my forefathers. He said: If you are a liar, may God change you to that state in which you had been.

He then came to the one who was bald-headed in his old form and said to him the same he had said to the one suffering from leprosy and he gave him the same reply received from the one who was suffering from leprosy and he said: If you are a liar, may God turn you to your previous position in which you had been.

And then he came to the blind man in his old form and shape and he said: I am a poor person and a traveler. My provision has ran short and today I cannot reach my destination but with the help of God and then with your help and I beg you in the name of One Who restored your eyesight and gave you the flock of sheep to give me a sheep by which I should be able to make my provisions for the journey. He said: I was blind and God restored to me my eyesight; you take whatever you like and leave whatever you like. By God, I shall not prohibit you today for what you take in the name of God. Thereupon, he said: You keep with you what you have in your possession. The fact is that the three persons were tested and God is well pleased with the man who restored his eyesight and He is angry with the others.

Tale of the real estate

Abu Hurairah (May God be pleased with him) reported the Prophet (PBUH) saying: "A man bought a piece of land from another man, and the buyer found a jar filled with gold in the land. The buyer said to the seller: 'Take your gold, as I bought only the land from you and not the gold.' The owner of the land said: 'I sold you the land with everything in it.' So both of them took their case before a third man who asked: 'Have you any children?' One of them said: 'I have a boy.' The other said, 'I have a girl.' The man said: 'Marry the girl to the boy and spend the money on them; and whatever remains give it in charity.'"

Tale of the debtor

Abu Hurairah (May God be pleased with him) reported: The Prophet (PBUH) said, "An Israeli man asked another Israeli one to lend him one thousand Dinars. The second man required witnesses. The former replied, 'God is sufficient as a witness.' The second said, 'I want a surety.' The former replied, 'God is sufficient as a surety.' The second said, 'You are right,' and lent him the money for a certain period. The debtor went across the sea.

When he finished his job, he searched for a conveyance so that he might reach in time for the repayment of the debt, but he could not find any. So, he took a piece of wood and made a hole in it, inserted in it one thousand Dinars and a letter to the lender and then he sealed the hole tightly.

He took the piece of wood to the sea and said. 'O God! You know well that I took a loan of one thousand Dinars from so-and-so. He demanded a surety from me but I told him that God's Guarantee was sufficient and he accepted Your guarantee. He then asked for a witness and I told him that God was sufficient as a Witness, and he accepted You as a Witness. No doubt, I tried hard to find a conveyance so that I could repay his money but could not find, so I hand over this money to You.' Saying that, he threw the piece of wood into the sea till it went out far into it, and then he went away. Meanwhile he started searching for a conveyance in order to reach the creditor's country.

One day the lender came out of his house to see whether a ship had arrived bringing his money, and all of a sudden he saw the piece of wood in which his money had been deposited. He took it home to use for fire. When he saw it, he found his money and the letter inside it. Shortly after that, the debtor came bringing one thousand Dinars to him and said, 'By God, I had been trying hard to get a boat so that I could bring you your money, but failed to get one before the one I have come by.' The lender asked, 'Have you sent something to me?' The debtor replied, 'I have told you I could not get a boat other than the one I have come by.' The lender said, 'God has delivered on your behalf the money you sent in the piece of wood. So, you may keep your one thousand Dinars and depart guided on the right path.' "

Also, Tale of the two old women

Abu Hurairah (May God be pleased with him) reported: The Prophet (PBUH) said: "All wonders were occurred for Banu Israel. Narrated from the Children of Israel that there was a man and a woman from Banu Israel, mother of the man and mother of the wife lived with them. The man was in love with the wife and he was obeying her. The wife's mother was very ill-tempered but the man's mother was a good woman. The wife's mother made her daughter hate his husband's mother till she asked him to get her away or she will not do good to him except after having her away. Both two old women did not see. The husband did what his wife wanted him to do and got his mother away without food or drink to be eaten by beasts, then he left her. At night, prey animals approached her and an angel came to her and asked "what do you hear?" she said that she hears sounds of cows, camels and sheep, the angel said to her: 'Good, God willing.' And he left her. At the morning, she waked up and found the valley was full of cows, camels and sheep. When his son came to her, he asked: "O, mother, what are those? She said: "My son, it is the provision from my God." He carried his mother and had all what God bestowed her and when he returned back to his wife and she saw and knew what happened, she insisted that her husband has to take her mother to the same place to get the same as his mother. He set off with her old mother to the same place and left her. At night she heard the sound of prey animals and the same angel came to her and asked her about what she heard. She said that she heard the sound of prey animals were about to eat me. He said: "Evil, God willing." Then, he went away and left her. After that there was a prey animal came to her and ate it. In the morning, the wife asked her husband to go to her mother and see what happened to her, he did but he found nothing of her except her bones that the prey animal left. He went back to his wife and told her and put the bones of her mother before her. She felt very sorrow till she died out of grief.

Tale of the worshipper and the pomegranate

It is narrated that there was a man who worshipped God for 500 years on a mount that it was surrounded by water from all sides. God made for him a spring of sweet water and a pomegranate tree that was giving him pomegranate every day to be fed. He used to eat the pomegranate every day, drink water and wash for ablution, then pray to God. He asked his God to let him die while prostrating and let earth and anything be away from him till he was resurrected as prostrating. When God resurrected him and God says: "Take My servant to the Heaven upon My mercy!" He says: "O Lord, upon my work." God said: "Take My servant to the Heaven upon My mercy!" He says: "O Lord, By upon work." For the third time, God says: "Take My servant to the Heaven upon My mercy!" He says: "O Lord, By upon work."

God said to the Angels "set account for the deeds of My servant comparing to the blessing of the sight", the sight only equaled the worshipping of 500 years and the whole body surely is more then. Then, God says: "Take My servant to the Fire!? While he was taken to the Fire, he said: "O Lord, let me enter the Heaven upon Your mercy. God says: "My servant, I created you and you were nothing! Is this by your deeds or by My mercy?" He says: "It is by Your mercy, my Lord." God says: "Who gives you strength to worship Me for 500 years!?" He says: "You, my Lord!" God says: "Who gave you sweet water and granted you a pomegranate every day. You asked Me to seize your soul while you're prostrating!? "God says: "Take My servant to the Heaven upon my mercy."

A worshipper monk

There was a worshipper from Banu Israel who was worshipping God for many years in his hermitage and living in a poor state, devils complained to Satan that he was too hard to be tempted. Satan decided to work on him, himself. Satan went and knocked the door of his hermitage asking to stay that night with him. The worshipper said there were many near villages where the guest can stay. Satan said 'fear God and open the door, I fear thieves and wild beasts.' He did not open the door for him. Then, Satan knocked the door again and said that he was Jesus. The worshipper said if you were Jesus, so you did not need anything; you delivered all messages of your Lord.

Satan waited for some time then he knocked the door again and said that he was Satan, the worshipper did not open for him first but Satan insisted on getting in saying I would not hurt you ever. The worshipper opened the door for him and Satan got in and asked the Worshipper what was the easiest way to destroy children of Adam. The worshipper said that it was drunkenness. Satan asked: what else? The worshipper replied: "anger" . Satan said: and what? The worshipper said: 'stinginess'; withholding the right of God in their property, then it ruined.

Two brother worshippers from Banu Israel

It is said that there were two brothers from Banu Israel who went out for worshipping and while they were before crossroads, one of them said to the other to take that road and the other would take the other road and they would meet at beginning of the year. They went out to worship God and when they were approaching the beginning of the year, they met together in the same place. One of them said to the other one: What the greatest sin did you commit? The second said: "While I was walking, I found an ear of wheat and I put it in one of the lands, on the right and left, I did not know whether the land I put was the right one." The second one asked the first the same question, the first said: "While I was praying, sometimes stand on a leg for a time and the other leg for a time and I did not know if I was fair to them or not. Their father heard them and supplicated God: "If they are honest, let them die." Then, they died.

Three worshippers of Banu Israel

It is said that three worshippers from Banu Israel met together; they said "Let's mention the worst sin we have ever done?" One of them said: 'Once, I was with a friend, then I hid behind a tree and suddenly appeared before him, he was very frightened saying 'May God judge us'.

Another one said if one of Banu Israel was happened and touched with a urine, he cut that affected part, I was touched with urine but I did not cut it all.

The third one said: "There was a mother that called me and I replied but she did not hear me because of wind, She threw me with stones as she was very angry, I got a stick and went to her to beat me with but she feared me running and she hit a tree that cut her face, that was the worst sin I committed.

A worshipper from Banu Israel

It is said that there was a worshipper from Banu Israel who and his family did not eat anything for 7 days, his wife asked him to go out to find them something. He went out and stood next to the workers, they were all hired except for him so he said: 'I will work today with my Lord' he went to the river and washed and stayed the day kneeling and prostrating till the night and returned to his family. His wife said to him what did you do? I worked with my teacher and he promised to give my fare tomorrow. Next morning, he went out and stood next to the workers, they were all hired except for him so he said: 'I will work today with my Lord' he went to the river and washed and stayed the day kneeling and prostrating till the night and returned to his family. His wife said to him what did you do? I worked with my teacher and he promised to give my fare tomorrow. His wife became angry with him and they stayed the whole night feeling pains of hunger. On the following day, he went out and stood next to the workers, they again were all hired except for him so he said: 'I will work today with my Lord' he went to the river and washed and stayed the day kneeling and prostrating till the night. He said where I had to go, I left my family starving, then he decided to return to his family. When he was near to his house, he smelt food and heard people laughing; he thought that he may be asleep. He approached the door, then his wife opened her arms and said that the messenger of your teacher came to us with dinars and flour and said if your husband came, said to him that your teacher was pleased with your work and if you exerted more efforts, he would give you much fare.

Tale of Yarch

It is said that Banu Israel were afflicted with arid time during the time of Moses, so they asked him to ask his Lord for rain. Moses said to them to go with him to the mountain, when he was about to ascend the mountain he said, "A man with a sin does not follow me." It is said that More than half of the people returned, then he said the same statement again. Then, they all turned back except a man who was blind. Moses said to him: "Did not you hear what I said?"

He said: Yes, Moses said: you did not commit a sin?!, he said: I know nothing but something I remember, if it is a sin, I return.

Moses said: 'What is it?' He said: "I passed through a road and saw the door of an open room and I saw with my eyes a person I do not know. I said to my eyes: 'You rushed to sin, so do not stay with me after that, I inserted my finger in it, if this is a sin, I will return." Moses said: "This is not a sin." Then he said to him: "Ask for rain for us." he said: "O Lord, what You have do not run out and your treasures are not destroyed, and you are not satisfied with stinginess. Send us rain now", then they returned stepping on mud.

Tale of a Repentant from Banu Israel

It is said that a man from Banu Israel committed adultery, then he went to a river to have bath in, water talked to him and said: "O man, are not you shy; did not you repent from this sin and said you will not do it again". He went out from water in fear saying: "I will not disobey God ever." He reached a mountain where there were 12 men worshipping God, Exalted is He. He stayed with them till their place became arid, they descended from the mountain searching for grass, they passed by the river, the man said: "I will not come with you" they said: "Why" he said: "There was who knew that I committed a sin and I am shy to be seen." They left him and went on, the river talked with them saying what your companion did?, they said that he committed a sin and he feels shy being seen by the one who knew his sin. The river said:

"Exalted is He, your companion has already repented, return to your companion and said to him that I love him because he repented and returned to God and worship God beside this river. The man came with them to the river where they worshipped God for a long time till the previously sinful man died. The river called them to wash him from its water and bury him at the banks so that he can be resurrected next to the river. They did and decided to stay their night at his grave to weep and on the following morning they would set off. They slept and while they waked up they found 12 trees were grown by the hand of the Lord beside his grave, so they decided to stay in that place worshipping God till they all died and buried next to him. It is said that Banu Israel were going to these graves to visit them.

Tale of Qasara (from Banu Israel)

Qasara loved a girl very much, she was his neighbor. Her family sent her for a quest in another village, Qasara went out behind her and tried to have sexual intercourse with her but she refused and said that she loves him more but she fears God. He said that he did not fear God. Then, he was turned to be thirsty till he met a messenger of God to Banu Israel who asked him about what had happened to him, Qasara said that he was very thirsty. The messenger said to him: let's invoke to God to give us a cloud that casts its shadow on us till we reach a near village. Qasara replied that he did not do any good to God to supplicate to Him. The messenger said "I would supplicate to God and you say 'Amin'". God sent them a cloud that casted its shadow on them and told the messenger about his affairs saying that the one who turned back to God has a place better than anyone.

A female worshipper from Banu Israel

It was narrated by some scholars that there was a woman called Sarah, who came accompanied by her 7 boys, to a king who was enforcing people to eat the meat of pigs. The king had the eldest son and asked him to eat the meat of pigs but the son told him that he would not eat from something that God forbade it. The king ordered his legs and arms to be cut, then each organ till he died, then, he ordered the next one and asked him to eat from the pig's meat but he also refused and said that he would not eat from something that God forbade, the king ordered a brass pot to be filled with oil and heated, then he ordered the this son to be thrown in it. The king called the third brother and ordered him to eat from the meat but he also refused and said he would not eat from it as it was forbidden by God, the king killed him. Then, the king ordered the following brother but he refused so he was killed too. The king killed each one of the brothers in a different way till the last one, the youngest. The king gave the woman time to re-think and convince her youngest to eat but she asked her young son to do like his brothers and not to eat from the meat that God forbade and the king killed him as well. Then, the king said to her if she ate just a piece of it, he would let her alive. She refused to eat and said how she could disobey God and live mourning on her children, so he killed her after them.

Punishment of the liar to Moses (PBUH)

It is said that there was a liar who was serving Moses (PBUH) and learning from him. He asked Moses to get back to his village and when he returned he started to tell lies about Moses (PBUH) and did not return to Moses. Moses (PBUH) asked about him but he found nothing about him. Once, Moses was sitting and there was somebody holding a rabbit by a robe who passed by Moses. Moses asked: "Where are you from?" he told him: from the village …, from the village of that liar. Moses asked him: "Do you know…?" he said it was the rabbit held by a robe. Moses asked God to be restored to his previous form in order to ask him about the reason behind that.

Tale of a whore

There was a whore that was very beautiful and she was taking not less than 100 Dinars to let someone enjoy her. A worshipper looked at her and he liked her much. He worked hard till he collected 100 dinars and went to her and when he was with her, he remembered his standing before God while he committed that sin. So, he told her let me go out and I would give you 100 Dinars. She asked him about the reason, he told her that he feared God, she said then be my husband and I would let you out once you promise marrying me, he said to her: no, till he went out. The, he went out to his village while she felt sorrow and repented. She went to his village and asked about him but when he saw her, he died. She asked about any relatives of him and people told her that he had a young brother. She went to him and asked him to marry her for the sake of her love for his brother. She married him and gave birth to 7 children.

Tale of another whore

There was a worshipper from Banu Israel who was worshipping God in his hermitage, some people asked a whore to go to him so that she can seduce him. She went to him and kept asking him to let her enter and have shield from rain and darkness. She sat beside him to seduce him. His soul wanted to touch her but he burnt his finger with fire, then he returned to his prayer but his soul adorned for him the adultery but he had another finger burnt. That action continued till he burnt his all fingers while the whore watching that till she died.

Tale of a young chaste

There was a young man from Banu Israel who was selling baskets. While he was selling these baskets, there was a woman that was getting out from a house of one of the kings of Banu Israel and asked the young chaste to enter to buy from him. When he entered, she closed the doors, then, daughter of the king met him with uncovered face and neck. He told them to buy some of his baskets but they told him that they did not ask him to enter for that but they wanted something from him. He said to her to fear God but she replied to him threatening him if he did not do what she wanted, she would tell her father that he wanted to do evil for her. He asked her to let him perform ablution, she ordered a maid to prepare water for him at the palace so he could not escape. The height of the palace was 40 arms. When he was at top of the pal- ace, he supplicated to God and said that he was invited to a sin and he chose to jump from the palace and hurt himself instead of committing the sin. God sent him an angel who helped him to fall on his foot. He supplicated to God and said "Send me a provision so that I can forsake selling baskets." God sent him golden locusts till he filled his clothes but he asked his God if that provision was from the provision of the world, bless it but if it was from my share in the Heaven, he did not want it. Then, he was called that this was a portion of 25 portions, the reward of his patience while falling from the palace.

Tale of ascetic king

It is said that there was a king, he thought about his kingdom and found that his rule was to end sooner or later and he was very busy, ignoring worshipping his Lord. So, he left his kingdom and decided to go near to the beach and worked to feed himself and give charity. He continued living that way till he was mentioned for the current king who asked his soldiers to get him that man but he refused. The king himself went to him to learn more about him, the man told him that he was … King of …; He thought of his affairs and found that each rule had an end so he came to that land to be free enough to worship his Lord. The king followed him and left his horse and they continued worshipping God and asked God to cause them die, then they died.

Tale of ascetic king's son

There was a king from Banu Israel who was given long age, much money and many children. His children had a habit that when they grew up they was wearing hair clothes, live on mountains and eat from the trees till they death, they all did that. He was given a boy when he was very old, he said to his children that he feared that this boy would follow his brothers' steps and be alone after the father's death. They built a great wall. Once, the son thought that there was other people behind that wall and he wanted to go out to have more knowledge, they told his father about his desire, the father feared that his son would follow the others and ordered them to amuse him, they did.

In the second year he insisted to get out and while he was walking, there was an afflicted man. He said, "Can this affliction touch me." They said, "Yes", So, he returned feeling distress. His father (The king) said to them to try to amuse him with anything.

After a year, he wanted to get out and while he was walking, he met an old man. He asked the people if he might be afflicted by that, they said, 'Yes' He said, "Your life is very boring". They returned and told the king who told them to amuse him with anything.

A year later, he rode and went out. While he was walking, he met a man carried on shoulders. He asked about that and they said he was a dead person and he could not walk nor speak. He said, 'Where are you going with him?' They said: "We are going bury the dead person." He asked, 'What then?' they said that it would be the gathering day. He asked them about the gathering day, they replied: "The Day when mankind will stand before the Lord of the worlds?"." "يَوْمَ يَقُومُ النَّاسُ لِرَبِّ الْعَالَمِينَ" (83:6), each one is to be rewarded upon his good deeds and evils. He fell on the earth and said that he feared that there was something he might not know. He asked his brothers to let him go. They replied that they would not leave him, but they had to bring him back to his father.

When his father saw him asked him about the reason for his fear. He replied: "My fear is from a day when each one would be rewarded for good deeds and punished for bad ones". He wanted hair clothes and told his father that he would get out at night. While he was getting out, he said that he wished that he did not think about life...

.

Tale of our prophet Muhammad (PBUH)

Tale of his kinship

He is Muhammad ibn Abdullah ibn Abd Almuttalib ibn Hashim ibn 'Abd Manaf ibn Qusai ibn Kilab ibn Murrah ibn Ka'ab ibn Lu'ay ibn Ghalib ibn Fihr ibn Malik ibn Annadr ibn Kinanah ibn Khuzaimah ibn Mudrikah ibn Ilyas ibn Mudar ibn Nizar ibn Ma'ad ibn Anan. Scholars do not disagree about such descent, until Adnan but after Adnan to reach Kedar ibn Ishmael ibn Abraham. Some scholars say that there were 40 fathers between Ma'd and Ishmael.

There was a period between Muhammad (PBUH) and Adam (PBUH) that scholars differ about it.

Some say that there were 4600 years, some say 6113 years. Others say 5500 years. It is said that there were 1100 years between Adam And Noah; there were 1143 years between Noah and Abraham; there were 575 years between Abraham and Moses; there were 189 years between Moses and David; there were 1053 years between David and Jesus and there were 600 years between Jesus and Muhammad (PBUH).

Tale of the fathers of Muhammad (PBUH)

Abdullah, father of the Prophet of God (PBUH) was the youngest child of his father. Abdullah, Azzubayr and Abutalib are the children of Abdulmutalib and the same mother called Fatimah bint Amr ibn 'Aiz ibn 'Imran ibn Makhzoum.

Ibn Isaac said that Abdulmutalib made a vow that if he gave birth for 10 sons he would sacrifice one of them.

He gave each son of them an arrow and ordered them to write their names on. Then he entered to priest of the idol and asked him to move arrows and pick up one of them to choose one of his sons to be sacrificed. It was happened and the choice was Abdullah, the youngest and the most favorable to his father. When he was about to sacrifice him, Quraish stopped him and told him to go to a soothsayer and asked her. He went to her, she asked him about the blood money. They said it was 10 camels. She told them to return and throw arrows between him and 10 camels and if he was chosen again, double the blood money till it went to the camels and the child could be saved. They did till camels were doubled to 100 camels and Abdullah was saved from sacrifice.

Abdulmutalib took him and went to Wahb ibn 'Abd Manaf ibn Zuhrah ibn Kilab, the progenitor of Banu Zuhrah, and married him to his daughter Aminah, the best kinship woman in Quraish, then.

Abdullah married Aminah and she became pregnant with our Prophet Muhammad (PBUH). Abdullah was the youngest son of Abdulmutalib, then, but there was 'Abbas who is older than the Prophet and younger than Abdullah.

Abdulmutalib

Ibn 'Abbas narrated according to his father and his grandfather that Abdulmutalib went to Yemen during the journey of winter and summer where he came to a man of Jews who was reading Psalms and looked at him saying there was kingship in a hole of your nose and prophecy in the other hole. He asked if he was married but Abdulmutalib said, 'No' The man said that when you return to Mecca, marry. He married to Halah bint Wuhayb who gave birth to Hamza and Safeyyah.

Why was he called Abdulmutalib?

Hasim ibn Abd Manaf went to the Levant trading, he passed by Medina (Yathrib) and saw Salma bint Amr; she admired him, so he proposed to her engaging then marrying her but on one condition that she would not give birth except while she was with their family, he accepted and married her. He went to the Levant and then returned, she became pregnant. He took her to Mecca and when she was about to give birth he took her back to her family and he went to the Levant but he died. She gave birth to Shaybah (Abdulmutalib) and she and her child lived in Medina. Somebody from Quraish passed by Medina and heard a child who said that he was ibn Hashim. The man asked him: "What is your name?" The boy replied that he was Shaybah ibn Hashim ibn Abd Manaf. When that man returned to Mecca he told Almutalib (His uncle) about that tale. Almutalib sworn that he must take him. He went to Medina and recognized his nephew. People told him if you want to take him, you had to take him without his mother's knowledge. He told Shaybah that he was his uncle and he wanted to take him to the people of his father, Shaybah Agreed. When they returned to Mecca, people asked him about that boy and he told them that he was his servant. Almutalib bought him a garment and wandered with him and people saying Abdulmutalib (Servant of Almutalib). His uncle delivered him the properties of his father.

Abdulmutalib inherited his uncle Almutalib the matter of providing water and food for pilgrims. This honor was inherited after his grandfather Abd Manaf.

Abdulmutalib was the person who dreamt of digging Zamzam Well and he was ordered to provide pilgrims water. Quraish asked him to let them be partners drinking from the well but he refused, then he accepted that later.

Abdulmutalib was called Abu Alharith; it was a surname because his eldest son was Alharith.

Abdulmutalib had birth to 10 sons: Abdullah (Father of our Prophet (PBUH)), Abu Talib and Azzubayr, their mother was Fatimah bint 'Amr; 'Abbas, Dharar, Hamza, Almuqawem, Abulahab, Alharith and Algheydaq.

Hashim was called Amr. He was the one who started the two Journeys of Winter and Summer for Quraish.

Hashim and Abd Shams were the grand children of Abd Manaf; some said that they were twin and their youngest brother was Almutalib, their mother was 'Atekah bint Nemrah Alsalmeyyah. They had a brother called Nawfal and his mother was Waqedah; they were masters after their father Abd Manaf.

Hashim assumed the matter of providing water and food for pilgrims after his father. Ummayyah ibn Abd Shams ibn Abd Manaf envied him and wanted to do like him. As a result, there was a dispute between Hashim and Ummayyah where Ummayyah went to the Levant and stayed there for 10 years.

Quraish used that Hashim ibn Abd Manf assumed the responsibility of providing water and food for pilgrims as Abd Shams was travelling before staying at Mecca. Hashim was saying during pilgrimage to Quraish: "O People of Quraish, you are neighbors of God and people of His House. Those days, there are many people coming to you glorifying the sacredness of this house, they are guests of God and they are the most deserving for hospitality. You have to be more generous to them" Hashim was spending much money every year to provide them water and food. Hashim was the first one who started the Two Journeys; one to kingdom of Axiom (Ethiopia) and the other one was to the Levant. He died in Gaza.

The first to die from the children of Abd Manaf was his son Hashim in Gaza, then Abd Shams died in Mecca and Nawfal died in Assalman in Iraq, then Almutalib died in Yemen. Providing water and food for pilgrims was for Almutalib after his brother Hisham.

Chapter

The honor of Quraish went for ten men with the beginning of Islam era; they were Hisham, Ummayyah, 'Abbas, Abd Addar, Asad, Taim, Makhzoum, Adi, Jumah and Sahm.

There was 'Abbas ibn Abd Almutalib, one of the children of Hashim, who was providing water for pilgrims in the era before

Islam and he was still doing that at the beginning of Islam. Abu Sofian ibn Harb had the flag of Quraish that was raised for the war.

From Banu Nawf, there was Alharith ibn 'Amer who was providing food for pilgrims. From Banu Abd Addar, there was Uthman ibn Talha who had the honor of providing service to Ka'aba.

From Banu Asad, there was Yazid ibn Rabi'a ibn Alaswad who was the advisor, leaders of Quraish were not to agree upon a matter except after he agreed upon, He was from the martyrs with the Prophet (PBUH) in Atta'if.

From Banu Taim, there was Abu Bakr Assediq (May God be pleased with him) who was supervising the matter of blood money and fines.

From Banu Makhzum, there was Khalid ibn Alwalid who was the head of knights during the war.

From Banu Adi, there was Umar ibn Alkhatta (May God be pleased with him) who was the ambassador of Quraish to any tribe in case of war.

From Banu Jumah, there was Safwan ibn Umayya who was responsible for making arrows.

From Banu Sahm, there was Alharith ibn Qais who was responsible for money that Quraish was giving to their gods (idols).

Abd Manaf

His name was Almughirah. It is said that Qusai had birth to 4 children; Abd Manaf, Abd Aluzza, Abd Aldar and Abd Qusai. His wife was Hubba bint Hulail

Qusai ibn Kilab

He was called by three names Zaid, Qusai and Mujame'. He was called Zaid but he lived his childhood away from his people so he was called Qusai (the secluded). He was called Mujame' (the gatherer) because he gathered Quraish tribes and became their leader.

He was the head of his people in Mecca, he was the first king of children of Ka'b ibn Lu'ai who had the honor of providing water and food for pilgrims and the flag.

There was no marriage concluded except in the house of Qusai. Also, consulting a matter was only occurred in his house. His orders were worked by Quraish while he was alive and after his death. His house was called Dar Alnadwa (Gathering place).

He was the first man to set a fire in Muzdalifah to be seen by pilgrims; that fire continued to be set before Islam and during the time of the Prophet (PBUH), Abu Bakr and Umar.

When Qusai became old, he gave his eldest son, Abd Aldar, Dar Alnadwa, the flag, providing water and food for pilgrims. Qusai died and buried in Alhajun.

Kilab ibn Murrah

His mother is Hind bint Surayr ibn Thalabah, he has two half-brothers Taym ibn Murrah and Yaqazah ibn Murrah whose mother is Asma bint Adiy ibn Harithah.

Murrah ibn Ka'b

His mother is Wahshiya bint Shaiban ibn Muhareb ibn Fahr. His brothers are Adiy ibn Ka'b and Husays ibn Ka'b

Ka'b ibn Lu'ayy

His mother is Mawya bint Ka'b ibn Alqeen and he has two brothers; Khuzaima and Sa'd.

He is the first one to so-call Friday because Quraish was gathered in that day to listen to the speech of Ka'b ibn Lu'ayy.

Lu'ayy ibn Ghalib

His mother is 'Attikah bint Yakhludibn Annadr ibn Kinanah. He has two siblings from his father Taym and Qias.

Ghalib ibn Fihr

His mother is Laila bint Alharith ibn Tameem ibn Sa'd ibn Huzail ibn Madrekkah. His paternal brothers are Alharith, Asad and 'Awf.

Fihr ibn Malik

His mother is Jandalah bint 'Amer ibn Alharith ibn Madad Aljurhumi.

It is said that Fihr was the leader of Quraish in Mecca when Hassan ibn Abd Kilal Alhimyari was coming from Yemen, he wanted to move stones of Ka'ba from Mecca to Yemen. He launched raids on people so Quraish and tribes of Kinanah, Khuzaimah, Asad and Gozam went out headed by Fihr ibn Malik. There was a great fight where Himyar was defeated.

Malik ibn Alnadr

His mother is 'Ekresha bint 'Edwan. And it is said that she is 'Atika bint 'Edwan. He has two brothers; Yakhlud and Alsalt.

Alnadr ibn Kinanah

His name is Qais and his mother is called Purrah bint Murr ibn Tangah.

Scholars differed regarding the name of Quraish.

First: It is called after the sea animal Shark (Qirsh) as Banu Alnadr are like the shark, the greatest sea animal.

Second: It is named after Fihr whose name was Quraish.

Third: It is named after Alnadr as he was called Quraish.

Fourth: It is named after Quraish ibn Badr ibn Mokhalad ibn Alnadr ibn Kinanah. It is said he is Quraish ibn Alharith ibn Yakhlud. Quraish was the journeys guide for Banu Alnadr.

Fifth: This name means gathering as Qusai gathered Banu Alnadr after a disagreement among them.

Kinanah ibn Khuzayma

His mother is 'Awana bint Sa'd ibn 'Elan and it is said she is Hind Bint Amr ibn Qais.

Khuzaima ibn Mudrika

His mother is Salma bint Aslam ibn Alhaf ibn Quda'a

Mudrika ibn Ilyas

It is said that his name is Amr. His mother is Laila Bint Helwan ibn Imran ibn Alhaf ibn Quda'a. His brothers are 'Amer and 'Umair.

Ilyas ibn Mudar

His mother is Alraba bint Haida ibn Ma'd.

Ilyas gave birth to Qam'a who gave birth to Luhai who gave birth to Amr who is the first one who changed the religion of Abraham and set idols around Ka'ba. He made Bahirah, Sa'ibah,

Wasilah and Ham. Also, he constructed 'Isaf and Na'ila to be idols. He came with Hubal from the Levant and set it as an idol. He set Manat at the beach of the Red Sea. Also, he Built a house for Al'uzza to go around like Ka'ba.

Muddar ibn Nizar

His mother is Sawda bint 'Ak, he has a brother called Iyad and two paternal brothers Rabi'a and Anmr.

Nizar ibn Ma'add

His surname is Abu Iyad or Aba Rabi'a. His mother is Ma'ana bint Gosham.

Ma'add ibn Adnan

His mother is Mahdad.

It is said that Ma'add was existing with Nebuchadnezzar while they conquering the forts of Yemen. Scholars said that Ma'add is from the children of Qedar ibn Ishmael ibn Abraham.

It is said that Ma'add, accompanied by twelve men launched raids on Banu Israel during the time of Moses who asked Moses to supplicate God to destroy them but God said to Moses 'Do not supplicate against them, they are My servants and there will be a prophet from their children whom I love him and his nation much."

Tale of mother and grandmothers of the Prophet (PBUH)

The Prophet's mother (PBUH) is Aminah bint Wahb ibn Abd Manaf ibn Zuhrah ibn Kilab ibn Murrah.

Her mother is Barrah bint Abdul Uzza ibn Uthman ibn Abd Aldar ibn Qusai ibn Kilab, her mother is Umm Habib bint Asad ibn Abdul Uzza ibn Qusai ibn Kilab, her mother is Barrah bint 'Awf ibn 'Ubaid ibn 'Udai ibn Ka'b ibn Lu'ayy, her mother is Qulabah bint Alharith ibn Malik ibn Hubasha, Umayma bint Malik ibn Ghanam ibn Lahyan is mother of Qulabah, her mother is Dub bint Th'alaba ibn ibn Alharith ibn Tameem ibn Sa'd. Her mother is 'Atteka bint bint Ghadera ibn Hutait ibn Gashm ibn Thaqeef and 'Atteka's mother is Laila bint 'Awf.

Scholars said that the Prophet had more than 50 mothers, none of them married a man unlawfully. Prophet Mohammed was born from lawful marriage as were his mothers and fathers.

Tale of Fatimahs and 'Attikas who gave birth to the Prophet (PBUH)

'Attika means the pure and chaste. Mother of his father Abdullah ibn Abdulmutalib ibn Hashim is Fatimah bint Amr ibn `A'idh ibn `Imran ibn Makhzum, her mother is Sakhrah bint Abd ibn `Imran ibn Makhzoum, her mother is Takhmur bint `Abd ibn

Qusai, whose mother is Salma bint 'Amerah ibn 'Umairah ibn Wadi'ah ibn Alharith ibn Fihr and so on.

The Prophet (PBUH) had 13 grandmothers called 'Attika and 10 others called Fatimah.

Tale of what happened to Aminah during her pregnancy with the Prophet (PBUH)

It is narrated that it is heard from Aminah when she became pregnant with Mohammed (PBUH), that she did not feel any burdening weight like other pregnant women. It is narrated that Aminah did not feel pains till she gave birth to him.

Tale of Abdullah's death

Abdullah was born 24 years after the rule of Khosrow Anushiruwan. When he was 17 years old, he married to Aminah bint Wahb but he died while she was pregnant.

It is narrated that Abdullah went to Gaza with a caravan for trading. When they finished, they returned and passed by Medina while Abdullah was ill. He told them that he would stay with his maternal uncles. When they returned to Mecca, Abdulmutalib sent his eldest brother Alharith but when he went there, he found his brother Abdullah died and then he was buried. Alharith returned and told his father and they felt very sorrow for him while the Prophet was still embryo. He died at the age of 25.

Tale of his birth (PBUH)

He was born on Monday, 10th of Rabi' Al'awal in the Elephant Year. It is said on 2nd and some said on 11th.

It is said that he was born 42 years after the beginning of the rule of Khosrow Anushiruwan.

There are many sayings about his birth.

It is said that he (PBUH) was born in the house that is known by Dar ibn Youssef; the Prophet (PBUH) granted it to Uqil ibn Abu Talib but when he died, his son bought it to Mohammed ibn Youssef who built a house called Dar Ibn Youssef.

Tale of what happened after Aminah gave birth to the Prophet (PBUH)

It is narrated that while giving birth to the Prophet (PBUH), there was light in everywhere.

It is said that when he was born, he was sitting on his knees and looking to the sky. There was a man from Jews in Mecca during his birth, who asked: "O Quraish, is there a baby born at night? They said we did not know. They asked their people and it was said that Abdulmutalib had birth to a boy. When they told the

Jewish man, he said that the Prophecy was transferred from Banu Israel.

It is narrated that the Prophet said "while my mother giving birth to me, she saw that there was light that got out from her and lighted the places of the Levant."

It is narrated that when Abdulmutalib was told of the birth of Mohammed and what happened and seen during his birth, he took him (PBUH) and entered Ka'ba and supplicated to God, thanking him.

Tale of events that happened during the night of his birth (PBUH)

It is narrated that during the night of his birth (PBUH), Iwan of Khosrow (Taq Kasra) quacked and there were 14 balconies were fallen, the water of Sawa Lake was decreased and the fire of the Persians was extinguished 1000 years after being set. The king had meeting with his men in the morning and they talked about what they saw in their dreams and what happened at night. Mubazan (Persian scholar) said to the king that there was an event or something that occurred with Arabs.

It is narrated that the Prophet (PBUH) said: "I am Muhammad, Ahmad. Muqaffi (the last in succession), the Prophet of repentance, and the Prophet of Mercy."

Jubayr ibn Mutim narrated that the Prophet (PBUH) said: "I have five names. I am Muhammad. I am Ahmad. I am al-Mahi (the effacer), by whom God effaces kufr. I am al-Hashir (the gatherer), before whom people will be gathered. I am al-Aqib (the last)."

Some of his names (PBUH): The Prophet of repentance, the Prophet of Mercy, Prophet of Wars, the Witness, the bringer of good tidings, the one who trust in God, the Conqueror, the Trustworthy and the Last Prophet.

Tale of the features of the Prophet (PBUH)

It is said that he was moderately tall, shining with straight hair. It is narrated from Ibrahim ibn Muhammad who is from the sons (grandsons of Ali, that whenever Ali portrayed the noble characteristics of the Prophet (PBUH), he used to say: "The Prophet (PBUH) was neither very tall nor short, but of a medium stature among people. His hair was neither very curly nor very straight, but had a slight wave in it. He did not have a big body nor a round face, but his blessed face was slightly round (meaning he did not have a fully round face nor a fully elongated face, bur in between the two). The complexion of the Prophet (PBUH) was white with redness in it. The blessed eyes of the Prophet (PBUH) were extremely black. His eyelashes were long. The joints of the body (e.g. elbows and knees etc.) were large, likewise the portion between the two shoulders was broad and fully fleshed. There was no hair (more than normal) on his body. (Some people have plentiful hair on their body. The Prophet (PBUH) did not have hair on the parts of his body, besides places like the arms and legs etc.) He had a thin line of hair running from the chest to the navel. The hands and feet of The Prophet (PBUH) were fully fleshed. When he walked, he lifted his legs with vigor, as if he were descending to a low-lying place. When he addressed a person he turned his whole body towards that person. (He did not only turn his face towards the person he addressed, as this is considered impolite, and sometimes, it even denotes pride. The Prophet (PBUH) faced the person he spoke to, with his chest and body. The seal of prophethood was situated between his shoulders. He was a last of all prophets. He was the most generous and the most truthful. He was the most kind-hearted and belonged to the noblest family. (It means his character, family back-ground and everything else was of the best). Any person who saw him suddenly would become awe-inspired. The Prophet (PBUH) had such a great personality and dignity, that the person who saw him for the first time, because of his awe-inspiring personality, would be overcome with a feeling of profound respect. Anyone who came in close contact with him, and knew his excellent character was smitten with the love of his excellent attributes. Anyone who described his noble features can only say: "I have not seen anyone like the Prophet (PBUH) neither before nor after him."

It is narrated that a Jewish said that he had seen every described features in Torah for the Prophet. He lent the Prophet 30 Dinars for a certain period and left him and when there was a day before meeting his debt he went to the Prophet and said, 'Give me my money, You, Abdulmutalib's clan, are people delaying meeting debts." Umar talked to him badly but the Prophet (PBUH) said to Umar that he should have helped him having his dues and asked the prophet to pay the debt. The Prophet said to the Jewish man that the date of his debt would be tomorrow and said to Umar to take him and give him from the dates till he became satisfied. The Jewish person said that his bad talk to him resulted nothing except leniency. When the Jewish man received his dues, he entered Islam and said to Umar that he tested all features of the Prophet in Torah except leniency, which he found it extra in the Prophet's character and wanted to test him. It is said that the whole family of the Jewish man entered to Islam.

Abdullah bin `Amr ibn Al-As narrated that the Prophet was described in Torah in the same description in Quran, Exalted is he says: "O Prophet, indeed We have sent you as a witness and a bringer of good tidings and a warner"." يَا أَيُّهَا النَّبِيُّ إِنَّا أَرْسَلْنَاكَ شَاهِدًا وَمُبَشِّرًا وَنَذِيرًا" (45:33), the Qur'an, repeats what is in the Torah thus:

'Verily We have sent you (O Muhammad) as a witness, as a bringer of glad tidings and as a warner, and as a protector for the illiterates (i.e., the Arabs.) You are my slave and My Apostle, and I have named you Al-Mutawakkil (one who depends upon God). You are neither hard-hearted nor of fierce character, nor one who shouts in the markets. You do not return evil for evil, but excuse and forgive. God will not take you unto Him till He guides through you a crocked (curved) nation on the right path by causing them to say: "None has the right to be worshipped but God." With such a statement He will cause to open blind eyes, deaf ears and hardened hearts.'.   .

Tale of Events that happened during the 1st year after his birth (PBUH)

The greatest event that happened during the year after his birth (PBUH) was the Tale of the Elephant.

There was the war of Jeblah that occurred in the Elephant Year.

From the events; Thuwaybah was the first nurse of the Prophet (PBUH); She is also known as Thuwaybah Alislamiah. She breatfed the Prophet for days before Halimah bint Abi Dhuayb (Halimah Alsa'diyah). Halimah Alsa'diyah was the foster-mother of the Prophet (PBUH), her husband was from the tribe of Sa'd ibn Bakr, Abdullah ibn Abd Aluzza ibn Refa'ah.

Names of his foster-siblings (PBUH): Abdullah ibn Alharith, Anisah bint Alharith and Judamah bint Alharith (Alshaima').

When the daughter of his uncle Hamza was chosen to marry the Prophet (PBUH). The Prophet said: "She would not have been lawful for me, for she is the daughter of my foster-brother (Hamza), for Thuwaiba had breastfed me and her father."

Thuwaybah was the slave maid of Abu Lahab.

Hadith Halimah

Aminah bint Wahb went out with women from Banu Sa'd; the women within the tribe of Banu Sa'd were wet nurses. They would take the children of Mecca to the desert and teach them the classical Arabic in return for a salary from the family of the child in Mecca. She went with her husband and had nothing, they had a child weeping from hunger all the night and she did not have milk enough for him. No one of women would take him to her because the Prophet was orphan he had no family to pay for the care. Halimah felt sad that every woman had received a child except her. So she told her husband Alharith "By God it is oppressive to me to return to my companions without a new infant to nurse. I shall go back and take the orphan boy and accept him." Her husband replied "There would be no blame if you did so, as that God may bless us for such." Blessing came to her and family.

Her husband's flock during a time of great starvation was still healthy and producing milk while the rest of the people's were fading. A strange event happened when he was 2 years old. Muhammad's foster brother was playing with him then suddenly Halimah and husband saw their son (Muhammad's foster brother) came running back shouting, he said "Two men dressed in white grabbed my brother and cut his chest." So then Halimah and Al-Harith ran to Muhammad and found him pale faced. When asked he replied "Two men came and opened my chest and I do not know what they did." Consequently, Halimah took Muhammad (PBUH) back to Mecca and told his mother of what happened. Then she knew that he was special and would grow up to be someone great and extraordinary.

Halima came to the Prophet when he married to Khadija complaining from the bad conditions of the desert, she was given 40 sheep and a camel that she came riding it after the Prophet was sent as a messenger for God. She entered Islam together with her husband Alharith ibn Abd Aluzza.

It is narrated that there was someone who asked the Prophet about his first years and he said: "My foster mother was from Bnau Sa'd ibn Bakr. I and her son went out with the flock and we did not have food. My brother went to fetch food for us and I stayed with the flock. While I was alone, there were two great white birds coming to me. They started to cut my chest and got my heart out and cut it getting two black pieces from it and washed my heart and my chest. Then, they sew my heart and chest. They put the stamp of prophethood. They set off. I went to my foster mother and said what happened to me. She feared that there was something had hurt me. She took me to my mother and told her that she had to deliver me to her and told her about what happened but my mother did not feel fear and said when she gave birth to me, she saw a light that lighted the Levant". There are many narrations about the events that happened in the third year, that are very similar.

It is narrated that on Souk Okaz days, Halimah went to Souk Okaz (open air market) and took her son (the Prophet) to a sooth-sayer and when he saw the Prophet, he cried: "O Clan of Banu Hudhayl. O Clans of Arab, come to me!" People gathered and he said to them "kill this boy". Halima took him and hid him. People looked around and they told him: what boy? He said to them his mother took him and went. He told them that I saw a boy who would kill your religion's masters and demolish your idols and he would rule you. People searched him in Souk Okaz but they did not find him. Halima took her son and went back, then, she did not let him be seen by a soothsayer or anyone of people.

Halima went out searching for the Prophet (PBUH), she found him with his sister, she said to her mother that it was hot! His sister told her mother that he did not feel hot; there was a cloud that was casting its shadow on him.

These all what happened in the third year after his birth.

In this year, Abu Bakr (May God be pleased with him) was born.

CHAPTER 10

Tale of what happened during 4th year after his birth to the age of 38 (PBUH)

It is said that the event of opening his chest was during the third year and it is said that it was in the fourth year.

There is another narration that the Prophet was two years when he was weaned. When he was four, they took him to his mother visiting her. Halima told her about good blessings that happened to them because of him. Aminah asked her to take him back as she feared that he could be infected with Mecca epidemic. Halima went to Aminah and told her about what happened to the Prophet (PBUH), concerning the event of opening his chest. During that year, she was monitoring him and she found that as long as he walked, there was a cloud that moved above him. She was frightened as well, then she took him to get him back to his mother while he was 5 years but she lost him while she was on her way. She told his grandfather Abdulmutalib who searched for him but he did not find him. It is narrated that Abdulmutalib was who sent him to do something but he was lost.

Tale of events that happened during the 5th year after his birth (PBUH)

It is narrated that there was a priest of Mecca who came to Abdulmutalib while the Prophet was 5 years old. The priest saw the Prophet and said: "O Clans of Quraish, kill this boy, he would kill you." Abdulmutalib fled with him but Quraish kept fearing him after the priest's saying.

Tale of the events in the 6th year after his birth (PBUH)

The Prophet (PBUH) was his mother Aminah bint Wahb when he was 6 years old. She took him and went to his maternal uncles the Najjar clan in Medina together with Umm Ayman. She stayed with them a month. Umm Ayman found that there were people of the Jews and she heard them saying that he was the prophet of that nation. Then, his mother returned back with him to Mecca and when they were at Alabwa', Aminah bint Wahb died and was buried there. Umm Ayman returned to Mecca where she helped and served him during his childhood and afterwards in his adulthood.

It is said that when the Prophet (PBUH) passed by Alabwa' while he was going to perform 'Umrah of Hudaibiya, he said that he was allowed to visit the grave of his mother. He went to it and kept weeping and Muslims wept also for the weeping of the Prophet (PBUH), he said to them that the mercy of his mother touched him, so he wept.

It is differed regarding the place of her grave whether it was in Mecca or in Medina.

Tale of the events that happened during the 7th year after his birth (PBUH)

Guardianship by Abdulmutalib

The Prophet (PBUH) was with his mother Aminah bint Wahb till she died. After her death, his grandfather Abdulmutalib was his guardian and took him to live near to him and asked Umm Ayman to take care of him as he heard some people of the Jews that he would be the Prophet of this nation. It is said that there was no one very near to Abdulmutalib than the Prophet (PBUH). When Abdulmutalib was about to die he commended to his son Abu Talib the charge and protection of the Prophet (PBUH).

From these events that happened during this year

Abdulmutalib went to congratulate Sayf ibn Dhi-Yazanon being a king and Sayf told him a tiding that the Prophet of God would be from his children.

When Sayf ibn Dhi-Yazanon ruled and became king of Yemen and ended the Aksumaite rule over southern of Arabia. The most honored people of Arabs went to him to congratulate him. There were five men of Quraish; Abdulmutalib ibn Hasim was one of them. They asked for permit to enter to the king, he allowed them to enter. The king saluted them and asked them to stay with him for a month. The king sent to Abdulmutalib to meet him. When they met together, the king said to Abdulmutalib that he wanted to tell him a secret he knew. The king said that I found in the previous books and knowledge that there would be honor and pride for your people and you; there would be a prophet from your children, his name is Mohammed and Ahmed. It is a boy whose father and mother died and his grandfather and uncle will take care of him. He said to Abdulmutalib that he is his grandfather. Abdulmutalib told him about his son and the Prophet (PBUH). Sayf said that when he grew up, come and told me about his news.

Tale of events that happened during the 8th year after his birth (PBUH)

Death of Abdulmutalib

Before his death, Abdulmutalib commended the charge of the Prophet (PBUH) to his son Abu Talib.

There are three sayings about the guardianship by Abu Talib:

First: It was upon the commandment of Abdulmutalib.

Second: They drew lot and it was for Abu Talib.

Third: The Prophet (PBUH) chose him.

Abdulmutalib died when he was 82 years old while the Prophet was 28 months old. He died during the rule of Hormuz Anushiruwan and Qabus ibn Almundhir.

From the events: Guardianship by Abu Talib for the Prophet (PBUH)

When Abdulmutalib died, Abu Talib assumed the responsibility of the Prophet (PBUH) who loved him so much. He did not sleep except beside him (PBUH) and when he go out, he took him (PBUH) as well. Abu Talib and his children were not eating except while the Prophet was among them.

It is said that there was an idol that Quraish glorified and staying at it all the day, Abu Talib was attending it and he was asking the Prophet to attend it but the Prophet (PBUH) was refusing. His uncles and aunts were very angry with him (PBUH).

The event of death of Hatim Altai

He was Hatim ibn Abdallah ibn Sa'd Atta'iy, he was a famous Arab poet who belonged to Ta'iy tribe of Arabia. He was very big-hearted and known for his generosity.

Some events that happened during the 9th year after his birth (PBUH):

Abu Talib went to Bosra and took the Prophet (PBUH) with him while he was 9 years old.

Events during the 10th year after his birth (PBUH)

Alfijar Wars

They are from Arab's wars. The wars continued for many years. They are called Alfijar Wars because many restrictions were violated, during the sacred months.

First Alfijar Wars

The war lasted for three days. The first day was because there was someone from Banu Hawazin who cut the leg of a man from Banu Mudrikah.

The second day was when some young men from Banu Kinanah abused a woman from Banu 'Amer where there was a great killing among them.

The third day was when a man from Banu Gashm ibn Bakr had a debt on a man from Banu Kinanah, then there was a dispute between them resulted in a war among the two clans.

There was the event of traveling to Bosra with his uncle Abu Talib while he was 13 years old.

When he was 12 years, two months and 10 days old, his uncle Abu Talib took him and traveled to Bosra in the Levant. When Abu Talib was about to travel to Bosra, his heart was lenient to the Prophet and decided that they never be separated and took the Prophet with him to Bosra in the Levant. When they reached their destination, there was a monk was called 'Bahira' , he was very aware to Christianity. He invited them to have food with him when he saw that there was a cloud casting its shadow on a young boy. They went to him but the prophet refused. He found that the cloud was still above the tree they were sitting below. He told them I asked you all to have food, was there any one who did not come? They told him that there was a young boy sitting beside their luggage. Alharith ibn Abdulmutalib went to him and carried him and they let him sit among them. The monk watched the cloud while he was coming and looked at him carefully. After they finished having their food, he asked the Prophet some questions about some descriptions that found mentioned in their Book and the Prophet (PBUH) answered him. He revealed the back of the Prophet and saw the seal of prophethood and kissed it.

Abu Talib feared from the reaction of the monk. The monk asked him about the boy. Abu Talib said that he was his son, he said that the boy was not his son and his father was not alive. Abu Talib said that the boy was his nephew and told him about his father and mother. The monk said to him to get back to his people and to be aware to Jews, if they learnt about him, they would hurt him; that boy would have great position according to what described in the monk's Book.

When they finished their trade, Abu Talib went out quickly as there were some Jews recognized the Prophet and wanted to kill him. They went to Bahira and told him about the boy, he said to them "if you recognized him, then you would not hurt him." They believed him and forgot about the boy. Then, Abu Talib returned and decided not to travel with the Prophet again.

Tale of events that occurred during the 14th year after his birth (PBUH)

The event of the last Alfijar War

The last war was between Banu Hawazin and Banu Quraish.it is narrated that that war occurred while the Prophet (PBUH) was 20 years old.

It is said that the reason for the war is that there was a man from Banu Bakr killed a man from Banu Kilab. The two parties gathered at the time of Souk Okaz that it was not held during that year. Clans of Qays and clans of Kinanh were all gathered and fought against each other; there were many killed persons. At the end of that day the war ended.

Tale of events that occurred in the 15th year after his birth (PBUH)

In that year Souk Okaz was held after the war.

From the events that occurred during the 16th year after his birth (PBUH)

Preparation of dissenters against Hormuz ibn Khosrow Anushiruwan.

From the events that occurred during the 17th year after his birth (PBUH)

King of Turk went to Hormuz ibn Khosrow Anushiruwan, followed by 300,000 soldiers. Also, King of Romans went to Hormuz followed by 80,000 soldiers. King of islands and some great army from Arabs went to Hormuz, too. Enemies of Hormuz were bold and conquered his country. Hormuz went to Turk's king, killed him and defeated his army. One of his soldiers, Buhram, feared the strength of Hormuz, so he returned with his brigade to Almada'in and showed their anger and declared that his son Khosrow Parviz (the Victorious) is more qualified to kingship than Hormuz. They managed to kick off Hormuz. There were many disputes and conflicts between leaders of the army and Khosrow; there were wars against them that led him to flee to the Roman Empire seeking the help of its king.

Tale of events during the 19th year after his birth (PBUH)

The death of Hormuz ibn Khosrow Anushiruwan; his rule lasted for 11 years and 7 months and it is said that it lasted for 12 years.

During that year: His son, Khosrow Parviz (the Victorious), assumed the rule and he was the most oppressive king.

Tale of Shirin

Biographers said that Shirin was born in Almada'in. When Purviz was young, he used to get in the house, where she was staying with an honorable man. One day, Purviz gave her a ring that she took it. The man was asked her not to appear before him again. He ordered one of his servants to take her and cause her die. She agreed with that servant to leave her alive and she would disappear. The servant went to the man and told him he saw her dying. She went to one of the monasteries and lived there.

Once, Purviz settled ruling after his father. She asked someone about him and gave him the ring. He went to Purviz and told him about her place. Purviz was pleased so much and sent a messenger who fetched her and they married. She was very beautiful and perfect. They made a covenant that no one of them would marry again if one of them died. After Purviz had died, Kavad II wanted to marry her but she refused and told him about the covenants. He took her fields and properties. When she found that her properties would be lost, she told him that she would accept his proposal but after three requests. She asked him to get her properties and fields back, hand her killers of her husband and collect people and told them about his lies regarding committing adultery with her. He met her requests, she restored her properties and murdered the killers of her husband, then she committed suicide. Kavad II felt very sorrow and was very sad for her.

From these events, some scholars said, Alfijar War II.

Also, Hilf al-Fudul (League of the Virtuous) was an alliance created by the Islamic Prophet Muhammad and various Meccans, to establish justice for all, through collective action, even for those who had no connections to the powerful. It is said that its reason was that Quraish was appealing in Haram. Once, Abdullah ibn Gad'an and Azzubair ibn Abdulmuttalib called for the alliance and achieving justice, Banu Hashim, Banu Zuhrah and Banu Taim met in the house of Abdullah ibn Gad'an.

There were no events to be mentioned in years 21, 22, 23 and 24.

Tale of events during the 25th year after his birth (PBUH)

He got out to the Levant for the second time for trading for Khadija bint Khuwaylid and married to her.

It is said that when the Prophet was 25 years old, Abu Talib said to him that he was a poor man and there were camels of his people were getting out to the Levant. Khadija bint Khuwaylid sent people from his clan with her camels. She learnt about that and sent to the Prophet that she would give him double what she used to pay for others.

Abu Talib said to him that it was a provision, sent to you. The Prophet (PBUH) together with Maisarah went to Busra in the Levant. They sat under the shadow of a tree where Nastour the Monk saw him and said to Maisarah that he was a prophet. Then, it happened that there was a dispute between the Prophet (PBUH) and a man who asked him to swear with Allat and Aluzza. The Prophet (PBUH) said that he did not ever swear with them and when he was passing by them, he did not look at them. The Monk said to Maisarah that he swore by God that he was the prophet whose features mentioner in their books. When Maisarah realized that as long as it was hot, there was a shadow over the Prophet (PBUH). They sold their goods and profited double what they used to get. When they returned to Mecca, it was at noon and Khadija found the shadow over him. Khadija told her servant about what she saw and he told her that he watched that shadow along the journey and told her about the tale of Nastour the Monk.

Khadija was a strict, serious and noble woman from Quraish, she was the greatest noble and rich woman among her people. Every man from her people was looking forward to marry her.

Khadija sent to the Prophet (PBUH) when he returned from the Levant offering him to marry her and asked him to go to her on a certain day. The Prophet (PBUH) together with his uncle Abu Talib went to her asking her uncle Amr ibn Asad to let him marry Khadija. The Prophet (PBUH) married her when he was 25 years old and she was 40 years old.

Khadija had married to Abu Hala, his name is Malik ibn Nabash, and gave birth to two boys, Hind and Halah. Then she married to 'Atiq ibn 'Aidh Almakhzoumi and she gave birth to a girl called Hind.

Scholars said that Khadija gave birth to the Prophet's all children: Zainab, Ruqayyah, Umm Kulthum, Fatima, Qasim and Abdullah except Ibrahim who was born from Maria al-Qibtiyya. All sons died before the mission (Before Islam) but daughters were alive during Islam and they embraced Islam and migrated with him (PBUH) to Medina.

Khadija's house is where the mosque of Khadija; it was purchased by Muawiyah ibn Abu Sufian who converted it into a mosque.

It was narrated by ibn Abbas that the first son of the Prophet (PBUH), before being a prophet, was Qasim and the prophet was called Abu Alqasim (Nickname). Then, there were Zainab, Ruqayyah, Fatima, Umm Kulthum, then Abdullah; they were all from Khadija bint Khuwaylid ibn Asad ibn Abdul 'Uzza ibn Qusai. Her mother is Fatimah bint Za'idah ibn Alasam. First child to die was Qasim, then, Abdullah died in Mecca. It is said he was cut off, Exalted is he says: "Indeed, your enemy is the one cut off". "إِنَّ شَانِئَكَ هُوَ الْأَبْتَرُ" (108:3).

It is said that Qasim died when he was two years old.

Tale of events during the 32nd year after his birth (PBUH)

Romans renounced their king, Maurice, and passed the rule to Phocas. Then they killed him and his heirs except a son, who managed to flee to Khosrow who protected him and made him a king on Romans. He commanded three of his leaders, accompanied by great number of soldiers to go with him. One of them was called Romizan who turned to the Levant till he reached Jerusalem in Palestine. The second commander, is called Shahin, was sent to Alexandria, Egypt and Nubia.

The third commander is called Farhan who turned to Constantinople where Khosrow ordered him to destroy and devastate the Romans country but they must not abuse the son of Maurice and they killed Phocas. Romans were ruled by a man called Heraclius who decided to launch war against Khosrow.

When Khosrow knew that he sent a commander called Rahazar together with 12000 soldiers and told him to camp in a place but Heraclius managed to pass through Tigris from another place. Rahazar wrote to Khosrow informing him of what had happened. Heraclius marched till he was at Almada'in where Khosrow fortified in. When Khosrow was ready for facing Heraclius, Heraclius returned to Romans lands. Khosrow sent to Romans another commander called Sharabraz who dominated them and destroyed their cities.

Tale of events that occurred during the 35th year after his birth (PBUH)

In that year Quraish demolished Kaaba.

It is said that Kaaba was not of a great hight and Quraish wanted to make its wall high and construct ceil for it.

That was dated 15 years after Alfijar War, when the Prophet (PBUH) was 35 years old.

People feared demolishing it. Walid ibn Almughirah was the first one who started to demolish it, then when they found that there was nothing happened to him, they were sure that God was pleased with what had happened. People and Walid demolished it till it fell to the bases. They got stones and built it till they reached the place of the corner where there was a dispute aroused among them regarding those who built it. They consulted each other till they reached that the first man to enter Kaaba was the man to decide. It was the prophet (PBUH) the first one to enter.

They all agreed upon him. The Prophet (PBUH) asked them to get a garment, he put the cornerstone on it and told them that every tribe shall carry the sides of the garment. It is said that when it was raining, the torrent cracked the walls and they feared being demolished.

The Prophet was known among Quraish before the revelation of being honest.

Kaaba was built when the Prophet (PBUH) was 35 years old.

Chapter

In that year, Fatimah was born. Also, Zaid ibn Amr ibn Nawfal died. He was searching for the right religion; he went to the Levant asking Jews and Christians about their religion. A Christian said to him that he was searching for the religion of Abraham. He said: "What is the religion of Abraham?" He replied that it was the religion of monotheism and was very aggressive to those who worshipped idols not God. He replied that it was his religion and that what he knew. It was said to him that there would be a prophet from his people, so he must return to his people and wait for him. He returned to Mecca and when he saw a man who sacrificed a sheep, he told him: "God is who created this sheep and sent down from the sky, rain and brought forth thereby fruits as provision for you, then, you sacrifice it for other gods". It is said that Zaid had told someone that he was against his people and he followed the religion of Abraham and he was waiting for a prophet from the children of Ishmael but he did not think that he would live to that time and he believed in him as a prophet before he was sent.

Events that occurred during the 38th year after his birth (PBUH)

In this year, he saw light and he was hearing voice but he did not realize them.

It is said that the prophet (PBUH) stayed in Mecca for 15 years; 7 years seeing the light and hearing the voice and was 8 years under the revelation. He stayed in Medina for 10 years.

Tale of events that had during the 40th year after his birth (PBUH)

Khosrow Pruviz killed Alnoaman ibn Almundhir 9 months before the mission.

Section

Tale of signs of prophethood

The prophets were telling about the time of his mission and scholars of the Books were telling about his mission.

There were many scholars from Jews and Christians who were knowing about his features and that he was about to be sent and be the last Prophet of that time but some of them did not believe in him when he was sent; they refused to believe in him despite their description for him was come true. There were many Jews in Medina and they were always threatening people of Mecca that there would be a prophet who was about to be sent and they would take revenge from Arabs. But when he was sent, Arabs believed in him and they did not, Exalted is He says: "And when there came to them a Book from God confirming that which was with them - although before they used to pray for victory against those who disbelieved - but [then] when there came to them that which they recognized, they disbelieved in it; so the curse of God will be upon the disbelievers"." وَلَمَّا جَاءَهُمْ كِتَابٌ مِّنْ عِندِ اللَّهِ مُصَدِّقٌ لِّمَا مَعَهُمْ وَكَانُوا "مِن قَبْلُ يَسْتَفْتِحُونَ عَلَى الَّذِينَ كَفَرُوا فَلَمَّا جَاءَهُم مَّا عَرَفُوا كَفَرُوا بِهِ فَلَعْنَةُ اللَّهِ عَلَى الْكَافِرِينَ (2:89).

Signs of his Prophethood (PBUH): there was a great quake occurred in the Levant.

It was a sign that the monks were waiting for it; they were saying that he would be a youth and he was about to be old; he was avoiding adultery and grievances. He was doing good to one's kith and kin and commanding others to do. There were many Jews pursuing the news of Arabs to know when and where he would be sent. Jews and monks were waiting for his mission (PBUH) as they knew his features, names and he was the last Prophet but they did not believe in him and embrace Islam because of their arrogance, pride and envy.

Section

Tale of the events that occurred during the time of our Prophet (PBUH)

Tale of events that happened during the First year of his Prophethood (PBUH)

He was revealed when he was 40 years old and at the first day of his 41st; it was the 20th year of the rule of Khosrow Purviz. He was preferring being alone to worship God in Jabal al-Nour (Cave of Hira).

It was said that the Prophet was sent when he was 40 years old and a day. Jibril came to him at night of Saturday and Sunday. Then, he revealed him the message on Monday, the 17th of Ramadan in Cave of Hira. It is the first place where Quran has revealed, God says: "Recite in the name of your Lord who created. Created man from a clinging substance. Recite, and your Lord is the most Generous. Who taught by the pen. Taught man that which he knew not"." اقْرَأْ بِاسْمِ رَبِّكَ الَّذِي خَلَقَ، خَلَقَ الْإِنسَانَ مِنْ عَلَقٍ، اقْرَأْ وَرَبُّكَ الْأَكْرَمُ، الَّذِي عَلَّمَ بِالْقَلَمِ، عَلَّمَ الْإِنسَانَ مَا لَمْ يَعْلَمْ". (96:5). Then, he taught him (PBUH) Wudu (ablution) and Salah (Prayer).

It is narrated that 'The Messenger of God (PBUH) was asked about fasting on Monday, and he replied, "This is the day on which I was born and the day on which I was sent (with the Message of Islam) and the day on which I received revelation".

There are four sayings about the revelation of Quran.

One of them: On 17th of Ramadan.

Second: On 24th of Ramadan.

Third: On 18th of Ramadan.

Fourth: In Ragab.

Aisha narrated that: The commencement of the Divine Inspiration to God's Messenger (PBUH) was in the form of good righteous (true) dreams in his sleep. He never had a dream but that it came true like bright day light. He used to go in seclusion at (the cave of) Hira where he used to worship (God Alone) continuously for many nights. He used to take with him the food for that (stay) and then come back to (his wife) Khadija to take his food like-wise again for another period to stay, till suddenly the Truth descended upon him while he was in the cave of Hira. The angel came to him in it and asked him to read. The Prophet (PBUH) replied, "I do not know how to read." (The Prophet (PBUH) added), "The angel caught me (forcefully) and pressed me so hard that I could not bear it anymore. He then released me and again asked me to read, and I replied, "I do not know how to read," whereupon he caught me again and pressed me a second time till I could not bear it anymore. He then released me and asked me again to read, but again I replied, "I do not know how to read (or, what shall I read?)." Thereupon he caught me for the third time and pressed me and then released me and said, "Recite:

In the Name of your Lord, Who has created (all that exists). Has created man from a clot. Recite, and your Lord is the most Generous. Who taught by the pen. Taught man that which he knew not"." اقْرَأْ بِاسْمِ رَبِّكَ الَّذِي خَلَقَ، خَلَقَ الْإِنسَانَ مِنْ عَلَقٍ، اقْرَأْ وَرَبُّكَ الْأَكْرَمُ، الَّذِي عَلَّمَ بِالْقَلَمِ، ﴿٤﴾ عَلَّمَ الْإِنسَانَ مَا لَمْ يَعْلَمْ." (96:1-5) Then God's Messenger (PBUH) returned with the Inspiration, his neck muscles trembling with terror till he entered upon Khadija and said, "Cover me! Cover me!" She covered him till his fear was over and then he said, "O Khadija, what is wrong with me?" Then he told her everything that had happened and said, 'I fear that something may happen to me." Khadija said, 'Never! But have the glad tidings, God will never disgrace you as you keep good reactions with your kith and kin, speak the truth, help the poor and the destitute, serve your guest generously and assist the worthy, and the calamity afflicted ones." Khadija then accompanied him to (her cousin) Waraqa bin Naufal bin Asad bin `Abdul `Uzza bin Qusai. Waraqa was the son of her paternal uncle, who during the Pre-Islamic Period became a Christian and used to write the Arabic script and write the Gospels in Arabic as much as God wished him to write. He was an old man and had lost his eyesight. Khadija said to him, "O my cousin! Listen to his story." Waraqa asked, "What have you seen?" The Prophet (PBUH) described whatever he had seen. Waraqa said, "This is the same Namus (i.e., Jibril, the Angel who keeps the secrets) whom God had sent to Moses. I wish I were young and could live up to the time when your people would turn you out." God's Messenger (PBUH) asked, "Will they turn me out?" Waraqa replied positively and said: "Never did a man come with something similar to what you have brought but was treated with hostility. If I should remain alive till the day when you will be turned out then I would support you strongly." However, after a few days Waraqa died.

The Divine Inspiration was also paused for a while and the Prophet (PBUH) became so sad as he intended several times to throw himself from the tops of high mountains and every time he went up the top of a mountain in order to throw himself down, Jibril would appear before him and say, "O Muhammad! You are indeed God's Messenger (PBUH) in truth" whereupon his heart would be assured; and he would calm down and would return home. And whenever the period of the coming of the inspiration used to become long, he would do as before, but when he used to reach the top of a mountain, Jibril would appear before him and say to him what he had said before. (Ibn `Abbas said regarding the meaning of: 'He it is that Cleaves the daybreak (from the darkness)'. " "فَالِقُ الإصْبَاح" (6.96) that 'Al-Asbah' means the light of the sun during the day and the light of the moon at night).

Jabir bin Abdullah [may God be pleased with him] said: "I heard the Messenger of God – and he was narrating about the pause of Revelation – so he said in his narration: "I was walking, when I heard a voice from the heavens. So I raised my head, and there was an angel, the one that had come to me at Hira, sitting upon a chair between the heavens and the earth. I fled from him out of fear, and I returned and said: 'Wrap me up! Wrap me up! So they covered me." Then God, Most exalted revealed: "O you who covers himself [with a garment], Arise and warn. And your Lord glorify. And uncleanliness avoid"." يَا أَيُّهَا الْمُدَّثِّرُ. قُمْ فَأَنذِرْ. وَرَبَّكَ فَكَبِّرْ. وَثِيَابَكَ فَطَهِّرْ. وَالرُّجْزَ فَاهْجُرْ" (74:5).

People differed regarding who was the companion of the Prophet (PBUH) from the angels during the period of his prophethood.

It is said that Israfil was the companion of the Prophet (PBUH) for three years, then Jibril was the companion of the Prophet (PBUH) for 10 years in Mecca and 10 years while the Prophet was in Medina. Some scholars said that Jibril was the only angel companion of the Prophet from the beginning of the revelation to the death of the Prophet (PBUH).

Description of the Revelation

It was narrated from Aishah that: Alharith ibn Hisham asked the Messenger of God (PBUH): 'How does the Revelation come to you?' He said: 'Like the ringing of a bell, and this is the hardest on me. When it departs I remember what he said. And sometimes the Angel appears to me in the form of a man and speaks to me, and I remember what he said." Aishah said: "I saw him when the Revelation came to him on a very cold day, and his forehead was dripping with sweat."

Ibn 'Abbas told Shahr (ibn Hawshab), "While the Prophet (PBUH) was sitting in the courtyard of his house in Mecca, 'Uthman ibn Maz'un passed by and smiled at the Prophet (PBUH). The Prophet (PBUH) said to him, 'Why don't you sit down?' 'I will,' he said. So the Prophet (PBUH) sat facing him. While he was conversing with him, the Prophet (PBUH) stared at the sky and said: 'A messenger from God, came to me just now when you sat down' He asked: 'What did he say to you?' He said: "Indeed, God orders justice and good conduct and giving to relatives and forbids immorality and bad conduct and oppression. He admonishes you that perhaps you will be reminded"." إِنَّ اللَّهَ يَأْمُرُ "بِالْعَدْلِ وَالْإِحْسَانِ وَإِيتَاءِ ذِي الْقُرْبَى وَيَنْهَى عَنِ الْفَحْشَاءِ وَالْمُنْكَرِ وَالْبَغْيِ يَعِظُكُمْ لَعَلَّكُمْ تَذَكَّرُونَ" (16: 90) 'Uthman said, 'That was when belief was established in my heart and I loved Muhammad.'"

Events occurred during the time of being a messenger

Ibn 'Abbas narrated that the Messenger of God (PBUH) neither recited the Qur'an to the Jinn nor did he see them. The Messenger of God (PBUH) went out with some of his Companions with the intention of going to the bazaar of 'Ukaz and there had been (at that time) obstructions between Satan and the news from the heaven, and there were flung flames upon them. So Satan went back to their people and they said: What has happened to you? They said: There have been created obstructions between us and the news from the Heaven. And there have been flung upon us flames. They said: It cannot happen but for some (important) event. So traverse the eastern parts of the earth and the western parts and find out why is it that there have been created obstructions between us and the news from the Heaven. So they went forth and traversed the easts of the earth and its wests. when they heard the Qur'an. They listened to it carefully and said: It is this which has caused obstruction between us and news from the Heaven. They went back to their people and said: "Indeed, we have heard an amazing Qur'an. It guides to the right course, and we have believed in it. And we will never associate with our Lord anyone"." (72:1- "إِنَّا سَمِعْنَا قُرْآنًا عَجَبًا، يَهْدِي إِلَى الرُّشْدِ فَآمَنَّا بِهِ وَلَن نُّشْرِكَ بِرَبِّنَا أَحَدًا". 2). And God, Exalted is He revealed to His Apostle Muhammad (PBUH): "It has been revealed to me that a group of the jinn listened"." (72:1). "قُلْ أُوحِيَ إِلَيَّ أَنَّهُ اسْتَمَعَ نَفَرٌ مِّنَ الْجِنِّ فَقَالُوا".

Scholars differed regarding the first people to get into Islam; the most famous one is Abu Bakr; it is said Ali; some said it is Khadija and some said it is Zaid, May God be pleased with them.

It is said that the first man to enter Islam is Abu Bakr. From children, Ali is the first. From Women, she is Khadijah. From slaves, he is Zaid. Then, Belal, Azzubair, Uthman, ibn 'Urwa, Sa'd and Talha embraced Islam.

Events occurred during the year of his prophethood (PBUH): Khosrow Purviz's affairs changed.

Tale of the events that occurred during the 4th year of his prophethood (PBUH)

The Prophet (PBUH) was concealing the prophethood and was inviting people to Islam secretly. Also, Abu Bakr was inviting those who he trusted Islam. After 3 years of prophethood, Exalted is He has revealed: "Then declare what you are commanded and turn away from the polytheists"."

"فَاصْدَعْ بِمَا تُؤْمَرُ وَأَعْرِضْ عَنِ الْمُشْرِكِينَ" (15:49). So, the Prophet (PBUH) invited people to Islam in public.

It is said that the Prophet (PBUH) had invited people to Islam in secret and in public, some people responded to him, many people entered into Islam while the disbelievers of Quraish were not aware. But when the Prophet (PBUH) disgraced their idols and deities, they were hostile to him.

Ibn Abbas narrated that: "One day the Messenger of God ascended As-Safa and called out: 'O people! Come at once!' So Quraish gathered before him. He said: 'I am a warner for you before the coming of a severe punishment. Do you think that if I informed you that the enemy was preparing to attack you in the evening or in the morning, would you believe me?' So Abu Lahab said: 'Is it for this that you gathered us? May you perish?' So God, Exalted dis He, says: "May the hands of Abu Lahab be ruined, and ruined is he"." "تَبَّتْ يَدا أَبِي لَهَبٍ وَتَبَّ" (111:1).

It is said that when the Prophet (PBUH) invited his people to Islam, they did not respond to him but when he (PBUH) talked badly about their deities, they stand against him and prevented them from hurting him. Some of them went to Abu Talib and complained to him that his nephew (PBUH) disgraced their deities and they warned him, they suggested whether he would prevent his nephew (PBUH) from abusing their deities or he would allow them to deal with him and settle the matter. Abu Talib delivered a decent speech and they left him. The Prophet continued inviting people to Islam in public. The affairs became worse among them and the Prophet, till they went again to Abu Talib and said "we asked you to prevent your nephew from abusing our deities and fathers and if you did not stop him

(PBUH), we would fight him (PBUH) and you." Abu Talib told the Prophet (PBUH) about what happened and asked him to avoid . The Prophet (PBUH) found his uncle would not help and protect him, so he (PBUH) said to him: "if they give me the sun in my right hand and the moon in my left one, I would never stop inviting people to this religion or die for it." When Abu Talib heard what the Prophet (PBUH) said and wept, he told him (PBUH) that he would never force him doing anything and let him go saying whatever they wanted.

It is said that Quraish sent a man to Abu Talib asking him to prevent the Prophet from abusing their deities and they would not abuse his God. Abu Talib said to the Prophet (PBUH) that your people rulers asked for justice; they asked you not to abuse their deities and they would not abuse yours. The prophet (PBUH) said to his uncle that he was inviting them to the better for them; he asked them just to say a sentence that let them become kings and got all Arabs' favor. They said to him (PBUH) what was this sentence. He told them to say that 'There is no deity but God' they became angry and told him that they would abuse him (PBUH) and his God. They asked him to ask for something different, the prophet (PBUH) told them that if they gave him the sun and the moon, he would never ask for something else.

When Quraish knew that Abu Talib would never let him alone, they offered him a very handsome boy instead of the Prophet

(PBUH) who disobeyed him and his people; and abused their religion; their father's religion. Abu Talib refused and told them he would never abandon the Prophet (PBUH) whatever they did.

Disbelievers tortured those who got into Islam and followed Muhammad. God prevented them to hurt the Prophet (PBUH) through his uncle Abu Talib who gathered Banu Hashim and Banu Abdulmutalib and asked them to prevent hurting the Prophet (PBUH) and save him; they agreed and did.

Aktham ibn Saifi was a famous Arab king before Islam. He was one of the greatest wise persons; he was called 'Hakim Alarab' (wise person of Arabs). He lived for 100 years. It is said that he lived during the life of the Prophet (PBUH). When he heard about the Prophet (PBUH), he wanted to go to him (PBUH) but his people prevented him. so, he sent his son to hear from the Prophet and tell his father, his son told him the message of the Prophet (PBUH). Then, he asked his people to follow the Prophet (PBUH) but they refused. He decided to migrate to the Prophet (PBUH) but his people prevented him and killed his camel while he was traveling to the Prophet and took his water and food; he died out of thirst but he testified that he entered Islam. God has revealed: "And whoever leaves his home as an emigrant to Allah and His Messenger and then death overtakes him - his reward has already become incumbent upon Allah. And Allah is ever

Forgiving and Merciful"." وَمَن يَخْرُجْ مِن بَيْتِهِ مُهَاجِرًا إِلَى اللَّهِ وَرَسُولِهِ ثُمَّ يُدْرِكْهُ الْمَوْتُ فَقَدْ وَقَعَ أَجْرُهُ عَلَى اللَّهِ ۗ وَكَانَ اللَّـهُ غَفُورًا رَّحِيمًا" (4:100).

Warqah ibn Nawfal ibn Asad ibn Abd-al-Uzza ibn Qusayy Al-Qurashi died in this year. He hated worshipping of idols and he traveled asking for the religion and searching for it in books. Khadija was asked about the case of the Prophet and he said I found him the Prophet of that nation whom Moses and Jesus told about.

Tale of the prophethood episodes)

Migration to Abyssinia

It is known with the First migration.

When the Prophet (PBUH) told Quraish that he was sent as a prophet, they did not criticize him (PBUH) but when the Prophet (PBUH) abused their deities, they criticized and denied his message. They worked on hurting Muslims badly till the Prophet (PBUH) asked his companions to go out to Abyssinia. Some companions went out and some of them hid their Islam. Abyssinia, for Quraish, was a land of trading. There were eleven men and four women went out in secret till they reached the sea they found two ships which carried them to Abyssinia in Rajab in the fifth year of the prophethood. Quraish went after them to kill them but they lived safely under the protection of King Armah

(Known as Alnagashi). They went out during Rajab and they stayed for two months then they returned in Shawal. When Surat Annajm was revealed and the Prophet (PBUH) together with disbelievers prostrated, they decided to return to their people but their clans hurt them, so the Prophet (PBUH) allowed them together with many people to go out again for Abyssinia.

Tale of those who were born in Abyssinia

It is said that those who went to Abyssinia from Muslims with their children or newborns were 83 Muslims. It is said that they were 83 men, 11 women from Quraish and seven foreign women but when they heard about the migration of the Prophet to Medina, 33 men and 8 women; returned, two men died in Mecca, 7 were put in prison and there were 24 persons who participated in battle of Badr.

When Muslims went out to Abyssinia and Abu Talib protected the Prophet (PBUH) and Quraish found that they could not hurt him, they accused him of magic, soothsaying, madness and they said he was a poet, then they worked on hurting him (PBUH). Once they gathered around him (PBUH) when he entered Kaaba and told him that he was the one who was abusing their deities. He said 'Yes', one of them collared the Prophet (PBUH), Abu Bakr was there and tried to prevent that and told them 'Do you want to kill a man who says my deity is God.' Then they left him.

Ibn Abbas narrated that the people of Quraish gathered and decided that when they saw the Prophet (PBUH), they would kill him (PBUH). Fatima, daughter of the Prophet (PBUH), went to her father and said "your people gathered and agreed upon killing you." The Prophet asked her to get him water to perform ablution, then he entered Kaaba. When they saw him, they all lowered their sight and no one moved. All of them were killed in battle of Badr as polytheists.

It is narrated that while the Prophet (PBUH) was prostrating, surrounded by some of Quraish, `Uqba bin Abi Mu'ait brought the intestines (i.e. Abdominal contents) of a camel and put them over the back of the Prophet. The Prophet (PBUH) did not raise his head, (till) Fatima, came and took it off his back and cursed the one who had done this. The Prophet (PBUH) said, "O Allah! Destroy the chiefs of Quraish, Abu Jahl bin Hisham, `Utba bin Rabi`al, Shaba bin Rabi`a, Umaiya bin Khalaf or Ubai bin Khalaf." Abdullah said: "I saw these people killed on the day of Badr battle and thrown in the well except Umaiya or Ubai whose body parts were mutilated but he was not thrown in the well.

When Quraish increased their harm towards the prophet (PBUH), he was concealed in the house of Alarqam ibn Abu Alarqam.

When Muslims went out to Abyssinia, Quraish sent Amr ibn Al'as and Abdallah ibn Abu Rabi'ah to Alnagashi with gifts to let them catch Muslims. They went to the king and introduced their gifts, then they told him that there were some people dissented from the religion of their fathers and they innovated a new religion; they said that they were sent from their chieftains to take them to their clans as they were the most ones aware to their abusing.

The King asked that companions of the Prophet (PBUH) to come to him and he asked them about the religion they embraced and why they dissented from the religion of their people and his religion.

One of them was Ja'far ibn Abu Talib who replied saying 'We were people of ignorance; worshipping idols, eating dead animals, committing adultery, not keeping good relations with our kinship and relatives, being bad to neighbors and that was our state till God sent us a prophet from us, we know about his honesty and chaste, he invited us to worship God, Exalted is He, and abandon all deities that our fathers were worshipping. He commended us to be honest and sincere, keeping the trust, making good relations with kinship and relatives, keeping good neighborhood and keeping away from shedding blood. He prohibited us not to commit adultery, say the falsehood, take the property of the orphan and accuse falsely women of adultery. He

(PBUH) commended us to worship God, perform Salaah, Zakaah and Fasting and we believed in him and followed him. We obeyed him and worshipped God but our people were hostile to us and tortured us to enforce us to worship their idols. Then, we migrated from our country and we chose you and desired to live free under your rule.'

Alnagashi asked him to say some of what God, Exalted is He, has revealed. Ja'far recited verses from the beginning of Surat Maryam. Alnagashi wept and said that was the same as Torah and Gospel. Amr told Alnagashi that they say that Jesus son of Mary was a slave. Alnagashi asked them to tell him about what they said about Jesus. Ja'far said: "He is His slave, soul and the word that God said to the virgin Mary. Alnagashi told them: 'Go and live safely in our land.

In this year, Sumayyah bint Khabba died

She was a slave in the possession of Abu Hudhayfa ibn al-Mughira, Mother of Ammar ibn Yasir. She entered Islam and she was from those who were tortured in Mecca to abandon Islam. One evening Abu Jahl killed her by stabbing and impaling her with his spear. She is the first Muslim to die and become martyr.

Events during the 6th year of his prophethood (PBUH)

Hamza and Omar entered into Islam. It is said that they entered into Islam in the 5th year.

Reason behind Hamza's entering into Islam: When Abu Jahl passed by the Prophet (PBUH) while he was sitting near to Safa, he abused and told him hated speech but the prophet did not respond to him. There was a maid that was dwelling on the mount and heard what Abu Jahl said. When Hamza passed by the maid, she told him about the harm and insults that Abu Jahl did. Hamza became very angry and went to Abu Jahl and hit him with the arch and told him 'How dare you insult him while I was one of his followers?' Then, Quraish stopped hurting and insulting the Prophet as his uncle would protect him.

Reasons behind Omar's entering into Islam are three and we would talk about them during his Caliphate.

Events that had occurred during the 7th year of his Prophethood (PBUH)

One of these events was the event of Battle of Bu'ath.

It took place before the arrival of Mohammed, between Arab tribes of Medina (Yathrib), those of Banu Aws and Banu Khazraj while the Prophet (PBUH) was in Mecca.

The Prophet (PBUH) migrated to medina 5 years after Battle of Bu'ath. Some said that migration was 6 years after Battle of Bu'ath.

Tale of events that occurred in the 8th year of his prophethood (PBUH)

During this year: God, Exalted is He, said: "The Byzantines have been defeated. In the nearest land. But they, after their defeat, will overcome"." "غُلِبَتِ الرُّومُ، فِي أَدْنَى الْأَرْضِ وَهُم مِّن بَعْدِ غَلَبِهِمْ سَيَغْلِبُونَ" (30:2-3). There were many wars between Byzantines and Persians.

Caesar sent a man called Qatmah on the head of an army while Khosrow sent a man called Shahrbaraz on the head of an army where they met together in Busra. Persians defeated Byzantines, so disbelievers of Quraish were rejoiced and Muslims were sad. So God, Exalted is he, has revealed these verses. Persians did not have any book and they were worshipping idols while Byzantines were people of the Book. Byzantines had already defeated Persians after seven years in the same time of battle of Badr.

In that year, Quraish exerted much effort to stop Islam spreading and extinguish this light but they failed; Exalted is He says: "But God refuses except to perfect His light"." وَيَأْبَى اللَّـهُ إِلَّا أَن "يُتِمَّ نُورَهُ" (9:32).

Quraish continued their efforts; they wrote a document prohibiting marriage from Banu Hashim and Abdulmutalib and stopped trading with them. Muslims suffered much during these three years; they left Mecca and lived in the desert. This siege continued for three years; they sieged them at the beginning of the 7th year of his prophethood (PBUH) till the 10th year. It was tight as their children were crying all the day. Hesham ibn Amr ibn Rabi'ah sent them food..

The End

The End of Part 2